VIRGINIA

ART OF THE STATE

ART OF THE STATE

VIRGINIA

The Spirit of America

Text by K. M. Kostyal

Harry N. Abrams, Inc., Publishers

NEW YORK

This book was prepared for publication at
Walking Stick Press, San Francisco

Project staff:
  Series Designer: Linda Herman
  Series Editor: Diana Landau

For Harry N. Abrams, Inc.:
  Series Editor: Ruth A. Peltason

Page 1: *Washington and Lafayette at the Battle of Yorktown*, c. 1860–80. Artist
  unknown. *Abby Aldrich Rockefeller Folk Art Center, Colonial Williamsburg*

Page 2: *The Last Meeting of Lee and Jackson* by E. B. D. Julio, 1869. *The Museum
  of the Confederacy, Richmond. Photo Katherine Wetzel*

Library of Congress Cataloging-in-Publication Data

Kostyal, K. M., 1951–
    Virginia : the spirit of America, state by state / text by K. M. Kostyal.
        p.   cm. — (Art of the state)
    Includes bibliographical references and index.
    ISBN 0–8109–5562–8
    1. Virginia—Civilization—Pictorial works.   2. Virginia—Miscellanea.
I. Title.   II. Series.
F227.K67   1999
975.5—dc21   98–43100

Harry N. Abrams, Inc.
100 Fifth Avenue
New York, N.Y. 10011
www.abramsbooks.com

Untitled by Javier Tapia, 1998. The Peruvian-born artist has taught since 1988 at Virginia Commonwealth University, where many of the state's leading artists have trained over the years. *Reynolds Gallery, Richmond.*

"Good Old Dominion, the blessed mother of us all."

Thomas Jefferson

Before there were states—or even colonies—there was Virginia. To the English, coveting land across the Atlantic, all the New World had one name: *Virginia,* a virgin land. Almost half a millennium later, Virginia may be a fraction of her primeval self—but that's a mere matter of politics. The Old Dominion's historic eminence has changed not at all. She is the nation's birthplace, begetter of presidents (four of its first five), the unchallenged doyenne of good living and gracious hospitality. In this state, past, present, and future morph into and out of each other. Apple-blossom festivals and historic garden weeks, azalea queens and Civil War heroes cohabit with nuclear warships and high-tech sprawl.

The land itself deserves considerable credit for Virginia's charm. Before a European ever set foot here, Algonquian peoples had discovered the bounty of its coast—the wide, serene rivers, the broad Chesapeake Bay, the rich tidal marshes. England's first offspring on the continent, Jamestown, was born on the banks of such a river and soon prospered wildly from tobacco. Wealth from the smokable weed allowed the early planters to live like kings, their riverfront estates outfitted with European imports and worked by slaves. When civil war flared in Cromwell's England, many royalists fled to Virginia, and the mind-set imported by the cavaliers of Charles I flavored the class-conscious Tidewater well into this century.

Royalists gave way to rebels in the mid-1700s, when Virginians Patrick Henry, Thomas Jefferson, and Richard Henry Lee—to name only a few—

Mann S. Valentine and the Artist by William James Hubard, 1852. *Valentine Museum, Richmond*

led the verbal charge against British rule. Another Virginian, soldier–planter George Washington, led the Continental Army to victory, becoming the "father of his country" and its first president. Jefferson, the third, would influence the fledgling nation with his love of intellectual pursuits and of art, wine, and fine architecture; he also gave the state one of its leading institutions, the University of Virginia.

Leapfrogging on the Chesapeake Bay. *Photo Robert W. Madden/National Geographic Society*

Virginia's central East Coast location kept it at the forefront of American politics. A new federal capital arose just across the Potomac, its personality imbued by the Old Dominion's grace, its domed architecture a tribute to the neoclassicism Jefferson loved. But riding the cusp between North and South proved risky, and by the mid-1860s Virginia had become a battleground. For four years Rebel and Union armies surged back and forth across the state, so wasting her fertile lands that they, and Virginia's psyche, would take generations to heal.

With defeat, though, came change and growth. In Hampton, one of the country's most prestigious black institutions rose from the ashes of slavery: Hampton Normal and Agricultural School, now a university. Among its early students was the pioneering educator and former Virginia bondsman Booker T. Washington. Through the first half of this century, the state clung to its rural heritage, especially in the bountiful Shenandoah Valley. In the Piedmont, black sharecroppers worked the land in exchange for part of their crops, a harsh way of life that surely went into the brewing of their twangy, distinctive brand of the blues. And in the faded parlors of Richmond, novelist Ellen Glasgow watched and chronicled as antebellum society slowly burned itself out.

When the world went to war in the 1940s, the Old Dominion shook off its languor and became a hotbed of military industrialism. Virginia-born musicians Ella Fitzgerald, Pearl Bailey, and Bill "Bojangles" Robinson swung, belted, and tapped the troops into battle. Provincialism gave way to a new dynamism, and arts communities began to grow in urban centers like Richmond and Norfolk. In recent decades, creative natives have woven Virginia into their private visions. Writer Russell Baker captures the slow-moving, Sunday-dinner Virginia of his boyhood in *Growing Up,* while photographer Sally Mann—born in the house once owned by Confederate hero Stonewall Jackson—pushes the edge of her art with "new" images of the Old South, using photographic techniques from the late 1800s.

Today, Virginia is a savory blend of its tradition-loving past and its open-ended future. In the megalopolis that spills out from Washington, D.C., into northern Virginia, Hispanics, Middle Easterners, and Asians rub shoulders with descendants of the FFVs ("First Families of Virginia"). Internet companies flock here like migrating geese, making this part of the state a high-tech nesting site. Meanwhile, along the James River, plantations built by colonial tobacco barons are still inhabited by some of their progeny. And each November, a contingent of Mattaponi and Pamunkey Indians presents the incumbent governor with pottery, beads, and wild game for the state's holiday table—a ceremonial reminder of how deep Virginia's roots go. ✿

VIRGINIA

"The Old Dominion"
10th State

Date of Statehood
JUNE 25, 1788

Capital
RICHMOND

Bird
CARDINAL

Flower and Tree
DOGWOOD

Insect
TIGER SWALLOWTAIL
BUTTERFLY

Shell
OYSTER

Dog
FOXHOUND

Boat
CHESAPEAKE BAY DEADRISE

Cardinal and dogwood

Perhaps more than any other state symbol, Virginia's great seal captures the moral makeup of the state. The goddess Virtus—Virtue, "genius of the Commonwealth"—dressed as a warrior and bearing a sheathed sword, plants her victorious foot on the chest of a slain tyrant, illustrating the state motto. On the reverse side are Libertas, Aeternitas, and Ceres (for fertility), surmounted by the admonition "Perseverando." Designed by a group of prominent revolutionary Virginians in 1776, the emblem has been modified since then, but the message remains consistent: Virginians will stand up for their rights, be they individual rights, states' rights, or the rights of the nation.

Having established that, they can devote the other symbols to celebrating Virginia's gentler virtues—the spring glory

Oyster

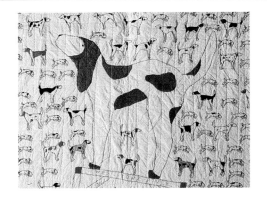

Sadly Songless

For decades, "Carry Me Back to Old Virginny" was the state song, but because of its antebellum theme and racial overtones, the state legislature retired it to emeritus status in 1996. Although there has been talk of holding a contest to choose a new state song, the Old Dominion remains officially songless.

of dogwoods in bloom; the sleek, well-trained foxhounds that lead the hunt; the old Chesapeake Bay deadrises, workboats of independent-minded watermen; and the succulent oysters, symbols of a bountiful bay. ❀

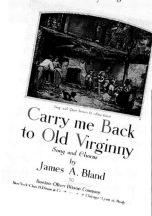

"THE VIRGINIA SEAL DEPICTS AN AMAZON WITH HER foot on the head of a tyrant. More appropriately, it should show a member of the League of Women Voters or the Virginia Federation of Women's Clubs presenting a petition to a legislator."

Guy Friddell, What Is It About Virginia? 1967

Above: "Carry Me Back to Old Virginny"—sheet music by James A. Bland. *Private collection. Above left:* Foxhound quilt, initialed "E. L. M." and "E. V. M.," c. 1950s. *America Hurrah Archive, New York. Left:* Pitcher featuring Virginia's seal. *The Mariners' Museum, Newport News*

Crab Imperial

1 pound blue crab
  meat (back-fin or
  lump)
2 eggs
1½ cups mayonnaise
1 tsp. Worcestershire
  sauce
1 tsp. salt
Dash of red and
  black pepper

Check crabmeat for
any shell fragments
and remove. Beat
eggs until light; add
Worcestershire, may-
onnaise, and season-
ings. Gently fold in
crabmeat. Spoon
into buttered baking
dishes—either indi-
vidual serving shells
or a baking dish. Bake
25 minutes at 350° F.

Capitol Ideas

Virginia's General Assem-
bly, the oldest lawmaking
body in the western
hemisphere, first met
in Jamestown in 1619. In
1699 the capitol moved
to Williamsburg, then to
Richmond in 1779. A few
years later, Thomas Jef-
ferson was asked to col-
laborate on a new capitol;
he worked with architect
Charles Louis Clarisseau
to design a classical tem-
ple modeled on France's
La Maison Carré. The

original building was completed in 1788, and wings
were added in 1904–6. A statue of George Washington by Jean Antoine Houdon occupies the place
of honor beneath the dome.

Left: Tiger swallowtail butterfly
(*Papilio glaucus*). *Photo M. H.
Sharp/Photo Researchers, Inc.
Above:* The state capitol,
designed by Jefferson. *Photo
Virginia Tourism Corp. Opposite
above:* Sir Walter Raleigh

"landing in Virginia," 1584, by
Howard Davie, c. 1914–44.
This illustration was probably
a romanticized fiction for the
English public. *Private collection
Photo The Bridgeman Art Library
International, Ltd.*

(Thus always to tyrants)

State motto

The Virgin Queen

The indomitable and officially virginal Elizabeth I was England's first monarch to encourage exploration in the unknown lands across the Atlantic. In the late 16th century, she granted her friends Sir Humphrey Gilbert and his half-brother Sir Walter Raleigh six years' rights to "all remote and heathen lands not in the actual possession of any Christian prince." In honor of his virgin queen—and in hope of her financial support—Raleigh named those New World lands Virginia. Although Raleigh himself never set foot there, the name Virginia stuck and in the early 1600s was loosely applied to a huge tract of eastern North America.

Virginia's legislature declared the American dogwood (*Cornus florida*) the state's floral emblem in 1918 and the official tree in 1956. For a small tree—usually under 12 feet—the dogwood is heavy with legend. Some Christians believe it became dwarfed after its wood was used to make the cross; Native Americans took the appearance of its white flowers as a sign to plant crops. Trees in bloom dapple roadside woodlands, most notably in the Piedmont hills around Charlottesville and the Colonial Parkway between Williamsburg and Yorktown. *Photo Carr Clifton/Minden Pictures*

Prior to 1570 Woodland Indian cultures flourish.

1570 Spanish Jesuits establish a mission settlement on what is now the York River.

1607 Three English ships land in the James River and establish James Fort.

1612 Colonist John Rolfe hybridizes a smokable tobacco for export.

1614 John Rolfe and the Powhatan princess Pocahontas are married.

1629 The province of North Carolina is carved from Virginia by royal grant.

1632 The province of Maryland is ceded from Virginia in a royal grant to Lord Baltimore.

1693 The College of William and Mary, America's second institution of higher learning, is founded.

1699 Seat of colonial Virginia government moves from Jamestown to Middle Plantation, later to become Williamsburg.

1716–18 First legitimate theater in the nation built at Williamsburg.

1754 Virginia troops under George Washington engage the French in the Ohio Valley; the French and Indian War is on.

1765 Virginia burgess Patrick Henry loudly protests the Stamp Act.

1775 Washington is appointed commander in chief of the Continental Army; Daniel Boone begins building his Wilderness Road through the Cumberland Gap.

1776 Second Continental Congress adopts the Declaration of Independence, written by Virginian Thomas Jefferson.

1779 State capital moves to Richmond.

1781 Lord Cornwallis's forces surrender to George Washington at Yorktown.

1789 Washington elected first president of the new republic.

1801 Virginian Thomas Jefferson becomes the third U.S. president.

1803 Virginian James Monroe negotiates the Louisiana Purchase; Virginians Meriwether Lewis and William Clark are dispatched by Jefferson to explore the new territory.

1809 Virginian James Madison takes office as fourth president.

1817 Monroe becomes the fifth president.

1819 The University of Virginia is established in Charlottesville.

1831 Tidewater slave Nat Turner launches a short-lived insurrection.

1834 Richmond-based *Southern Literary Messenger* publishes its first issue.

1841 Virginian William Henry Harrison becomes the ninth president. Harrison dies in office and is succeeded by his vice president, John Tyler, also a Virginian.

1849 Virginian Zachary Taylor, "Old Rough and Ready," is elected 12th president.

1861 Virginia joins the Confederacy; Richmond becomes the Confederate capital.

1862–65 The state becomes a major battleground of the Civil War, which ends with Lee's surrender at Appomattox, Virginia

1864 Pro-Union western Virginia secedes from the state to rejoin the Union as West Virginia.

1868 Hampton Normal and Agricultural School is established to educate African Americans

1895 Illustrator Charles Dana Gibson marries Virginian Irene Langhorne and models his Gibson Girl after her.

1907 The Jamestown Exposition commemorates the settlement's 300th anniversary.

1913 Virginia-born Woodrow Wilson becomes the country's 28th president and the last Virginian elected to date.

1917 U.S. entry into World War I makes Hampton Roads a critical military staging area.

1933 Barter Theatre presents its first season in Abingdon.

1947 Marguerite Henry's *Misty of Chincoteague* published.

1957 William Faulkner becomes writer-in-residence at the University of Virginia.

1962 Virginia-born Ella Fitzgerald wins Grammy for Best Female Vocalist.

1962 Dulles Airport, designed by Eero Saarinen, opens in Loudoun County.

1967 William Styron's *The Confessions of Nat Turner* is awarded the Pulitzer Prize.

1990 Douglas Wilder, nation's first African-American governor, takes office.

1994 President-elect William Jefferson Clinton begins his inaugural festivities by traveling from Thomas Jefferson's Monticello home to the capital.

1995 Walt Disney Productions releases the animated musical *Pocahontas*.

1997 Virginia Waterfront Arts Festival is established; hosts world-renowned performers.

1998 The exterior of Thomas Jefferson's private villa, Poplar Forest, is restored to its former Jeffersonian glory.

Striped by three distinct geographic bands, Virginia begins in broad Atlantic beaches, climbs through Piedmont, and ends in rough mountain terrain. The coastal plain that forms its eastern side is a level sweep of wetlands and sandy-soil pine and bayberry forests, cut by countless creeks and rivers. Lying in this plain like a vast shallow lake, Chesapeake Bay blooms with the sails of pleasure boats on weekends and during the week bustles with big freighters and cargo ships heading to and from the Atlantic. From the coast, the rivers reach inland toward their fall lines—where rapids and rock courses make them unnavigable. Here, the

easy roll of Piedmont hills takes over, gradually mounding into the low crest of the Blue Ridge. Beyond that gentle ridge lies the fertile swath of the Shenandoah Valley, famous for its apple-blossom springs and ripe golden falls. The valley's softness vanishes quickly as one moves west into the daunting Allegheny Mountains, which rise like a rampart down the long western length of the state. ❀

"HERE ARE MOUNTAINES, HILS, PLAINES, VALLEYES, rivers and brookes, all running most pleasantly into a faire Bay compassed but for the mouth with fruitfull and delightsome land."

Captain John Smith, A Map of Virginia, *1612*

Dismal Swamp by Flavius J. Fisher, c. 1870s. *Maier Museum of Art, Lynchburg. Opposite:* Great egret (*Casmerodius albus*) in Huntley Meadows Park. *Photo Frederic B. Siskind*

The Atlantic Coast

A discontinuous swath of sand—mostly quartz sediments washed down from its rivers over the millennia—Virginia's 120-mile-long Atlantic shoreline is indented by the yawning mouth of the Chesapeake Bay. North of the bay's mouth, the long filigreed peninsula called the Eastern Shore holds onto its rural, plain-spoken character. Roadside produce stalls offering corn, tomatoes, beans, and cantaloupes are backed by fields of green that stretch to the horizon.

In fall, those gone-to-seed fields and the abundant surrounding marshlands are populated by great flocks of migratory birds making their way down the Atlantic Flyway. The Eastern Shore's coastline—protected in Chincoteague National Wildlife Refuge and Assateague National Seashore—provides quiet havens for both people and wildlife.

South of the bay, the coast is more developed. Fast-growing Virginia Beach, its wall of high-rises facing the Atlantic breakers, claims much of the southern shoreline, its boardwalk always crowded and its beach blankets chockablock in the languid, humid days of a Virginia summer.

Above: **Sunset over Tom's Cove on Assateague.** *Photo Pat and Chuck Blackley.* **Right:** Horseshoe crab. Artist unknown, c. 1800. Horseshoe crabs have survived from prehistory; their eggs fuel the spring bird migration along the coast. *The Mariners' Museum, Newport News*

The Eastern Shore

From a glance at the map, this picturesque peninsula
would seem to belong to Maryland. But in 1608 an expedi-
tion led by John Smith mapped much of what is now the
Eastern Shore and its Chesapeake Bay islands; in 1614 the
Jamestown government bartered with Native residents
and took possession of these lands. The English first settled
here at what was called Accomack Plantation, which in
1634 became one of the eight original Virginia counties. In
1663 the region split into the two counties it retains today.

Above: Dunes at Dusk by Stephen
Fox, 1998. *Reynolds Gallery, Richmond*
Right: According to local legend,
the wild ponies made famous by
the novel and movie *Misty of*
Chincoteague are descended from
survivors of a long-ago shipwreck
off the Virginia coast. They still
roam the beaches and marshlands
of Assateague Island and Chincoteague. *Photo Michael*
Ventura/Folio, Inc.

Above: Crab buoys, used to mark pot sites, and oyster shells hold a kitten's interest on Tangier Island, Chesapeake Bay. *Photo Kelly/Mooney Photography. Right:* A crabber checks his pot for the bay's best delicacy—the blue crabs that proliferate in these warm, shallow waters. *Photo Lynda Richardson/ Corbis*

The largest inland body of water on the Eastern Seaboard, 195-mile-long Chesapeake Bay waters the coasts of both Maryland and Virginia, with the Old Dominion enclosing its southern end. Separating the Eastern Shore from the mainland and giving Virginia an extra 300 miles of shoreline, the bay is a capacious inland sea for pleasure boaters and fishers. Its shallow, tepid waters, only 20 feet deep on average, support schools of fish and abundant shellfish, particularly the famous blue crab. Technically an estuary—one of the world's largest—the bay is the drowned southern end of the Susquehanna River, its largest tributary. Four major Virginia rivers—the Potomac, Rappahan-

nock, York, and James—empty into the Chesapeake, as do countless small creeks. Hampton Roads, the broad inlet connecting the James to the bay, ranks among the world's largest natural harbors. Here, the Civil War ironclads *Merrimac* and *Monitor* had their historic clash; today the harbor buzzes with naval vessels and oceangoing ships.

Mary of Norfolk by George Tobin, 1795. The *Mary* was named for one of Virginia's greatest ports. Established in the colonial era, Norfolk is still a world-class harbor and home to the world's largest naval base. *The Mariners' Museum, Newport News*

"UPON THIS PLOT OF GROUND WE GOT GOOD STORE OF mussels and oysters, which lay on the ground as thick as stones. We opened some, and found in many pearls."

George Percy, A Discourse on the Plantation in Virginia by the English, *1607*

On the Shenandoah by William Louis Sonntag, c. 1860. *Christie's Images* Sonntag's image captures the romance of the Shenandoah Valley, still a pastoral paradise. *Opposite:* Fall colors in an oak woodland, Shenandoah National Park. *Photo Carr Clifton/ Minden Pictures*

Piedmont and Valley

Classic horse country, Virginia's Piedmont region gradually rises from the sea-level coast to tumble across the state's interior on a diagonal, southwest to northeast. Amid its fields of alfalfa and milo edged by oak and pine forests, gracious small cities sit at the fall lines of the rivers—places where the softer rock of the coastal plain lies lower than the harder upland bedrock. At the James's fall line, the state capital, Richmond, unquestionably presides, the regal arbiter of old traditions and new visions.

Farther west, pocketed between the Blue Ridge and the Allegheny Mountains, the Shenandoah—"Valley of the Daughter of Stars," as the old Indian name translates—owes its wide fertile lands to the snaking course of its namesake river. Its porous soils conceal a fantastical underground world of limestone caverns; in the north, both river and valley split into forks, interrupted by the long, low rise of Massanutten Mountain.

"ON A BROILING AFTERNOON WHEN THE MEN WERE AWAY AT WORK and all the women napped, I moved through majestic depths of silences, silences so immense I could hear the corn growing. Under these silences there was an orchestra of natural music playing notes no city child would ever hear. A certain cackle from the henhouse meant we had gained an egg. The creak of a porch swing told of a momentary breeze blowing across my grandmother's yard."

Russell Baker, describing a Piedmont summer day in Growing Up, *1982*

SOFT-FOLDED MOUNTAINS

Aerial view of The Homestead. The last of Virginia's great hot springs resorts, The Homestead has nestled into its own little valley in the Allegheny Mountains since the turn of the century. The well-heeled, including Vanderbilts, Rockefellers, and Fords, have come to recoup in its healing waters and equally healing scenery. *Photo Scott Barrow*

The Appalachian system that runs from Maine to Georgia blesses Virginia with two ranges; worn and gentled by 250 million years of winds and weather, they rank among the oldest mountains on earth. The eastern range, the Blue Ridge, averages 2,000 to 4,000 feet in height. Punctuated with rocky outcrops yet hardly rugged, the ridge owes its distinctive smoky duskiness to local atmospherics. In fall, its stands of oak, poplar, and maple provide a brief blaze of color.

In Virginia's far west, the Alleghenies form a much more daunting barrier, only occasionally breached by river or road. These peaks top out at 5,729-foot-high Mount Rogers. Straddling the border between Kentucky and Virginia, Breaks Interstate Park preserves the largest canyon east of the Mississippi. The Cumberland Gap cleaves the Alleghenies in Virginia's mountainous southwestern corner, wedged

between Tennessee and Kentucky; here, in the late 18th century, land-hungry settlers funneled through the gap on Daniel Boone's Wilderness Road into the great unclaimed spaces westward. Geothermal activity in the mountains has attracted more recent visitors to Virginia's famous hot springs.

The Natural Bridge, engraving by J. C. Stadler, 1808, after William Roberts. Colored aquatint. George Washington surveyed Natural Bridge and Thomas Jefferson bought it, calling it "the most sublime of nature's works." Modest Cedar Creek carved the natural stone arch, but the Monocan Indians believed that it was the "bridge of God." *Museum of Early Southern Decorative Arts, Winston-Salem, North Carolina*

"YESTERDAY I WATCHED A CURIOUS NIGHTFALL. THE CLOUD ceiling took on a warm tone, deepened, and departed as if drawn on a leash. I could no longer see the fat snow flying against the sky; I could see it only as it fell against dark objects. . . . It was like dying, this watching the world recede into deeper and deeper blues while the snow piled. . ."

Annie Dillard, Pilgrim at Tinker Creek, *1974*

The first humans to reach the mid-Atlantic coast arrived some 12,000 years ago, and evolved into the Woodland Indians who inhabited much of the East. By the time the first Europeans—Spanish Jesuits—attempted a settlement on the York River in 1570, the powerful Powhatan chiefdom, a consolidation of some 30 tribes, controlled the coasts and tidelands of Virginia. Their bark or reed-covered longhouses, called *yehakins,* clustered in small semipermanent hamlets, where the women and children tended crops of corn, beans, squash, and sunflowers, and the men hunted and fished.

With the English, who arrived early in the 17th century, the Powhatans had an ambiguous relationship: sometimes launching attacks, sometimes offering help. But the English were unambiguous in their ambitions. They were here to colonize, and within 50 years had destroyed the Powhatans' way of life. In western Virginia, people belonging to the Sioux linguistic group survived into the early 19th century, hunting buffalo in the Shenandoah Valley and warring on settlers who encroached on their hunting grounds. The only physical traces of these long-tenured cultures are occasional potsherds, stone tools, and, along the coast, oyster-shell middens that mark village sites. ❈

The Powhatan village of Pomiooc, drawn c. 1590 by a visiting Spanish Jesuit. Made for mobility, Powhatan houses usually had pole frames draped with reed mats or bark that could be rolled up in warm weather. Easily dismantled, they could be moved as the seasons changed. Powhatans thwarted the Jesuit attempts at colonization, rejecting the Christian God and massacring the priests. The tribe's own hierarchy of gods was presided over by Ahone, the creator, the destroyer. *Opposite:* A Virginia Algonquian Indian, probably a Powhatan, by Wenceslaus Hollar, 1645. *Both, Library of Virginia, Richmond*

"AT NIGHT, WHEN WE WERE GOING ABROAD, THERE CAME the savages creeping upon all fours from the hills like bears, with their bows in their mouths, charged us very desperately in the faces…."

George Percy, A Discourse on the Plantation in Virginia by the English, *1607*

An English Foothold

In late April 1607, three English ships sailed into the Chesapeake Bay and up a river they called the James. The small palisaded fort they built —Jamestown—would become the first permanent English settlement on the continent. Although the colony almost failed several times, in 1612 an enterprising Englishman named John Rolfe hybridized a smokable tobacco that would secure Virginia's fortunes for a half century to come. Rolfe went on to marry the Indian princess Pocahontas, who had befriended the early savior of Jamestown, John Smith. The marriage decreased tension between the Powhatans and the colonists, leading to the eight years known as the Pocahontas Peace.

In the legendary, and probably apocryphal, tale of heroism, the Powhatan princess Pocahontas saves John Smith from beheading. *Above:* In this portrait by an unknown artist, c. after 1616, Pocahontas poses as Lady Rebecca, the name she was called by the English. When she and John Rolfe visited England, she was taken ill and died. *National Portrait Gallery, Smithsonian Institution/Art Resource. Right: Smith Rescued by Pocahontas by H. Schile, 1874. Library of Virginia, Richmond*

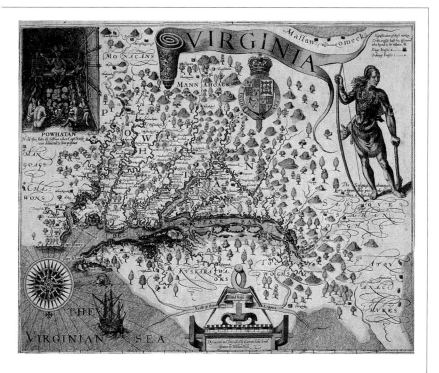

"When I think of Pocahontas,
I am ready to love Indians."

Herman Melville, The Confidence of Man, *1857*

Early map of Virginia by
John Smith, 1624, show-
ing in the upper right a
Susquehannock chief.
Smith mapped Virginia
extensively and, for his
day, accurately. *British
Library, London. Photo
The Bridgeman Art
Library International, Ltd.*

To the Manor Born

The nation's oldest working plantation, Shirley Plantation is still occupied by descendants of the founding Hill and Carter families. *Photo Catherine Karnow/Woodfin Camp & Associates*

The tobacco economy soon gave rise to manorial plantations along the riverfronts—and to the invidious spread of slavery. Although tobacco's heyday in Virginia was short-lived—as the crop so quickly depleted the soil—it left the Tidewater with an entrenched social hierarchy that mirrored the English class system. So loyal to English traditions were Virginia's cavaliers that during the Restoration, King Charles added Virginia's arms to his royal shield, making it his fifth dominion— affectionately called the Old Dominion. But all did not remain well between the mother country and her offspring. The imperiousness of royal rule grated on many independent-spirited Virginians, and as early as 1676 Nathaniel Bacon led a brief uprising against the royal governor.

In the mid-1700s, British forces arrived in Virginia to fight the French for western lands. Among the colonists to play a distinguishing role in the French and Indian War was a young Virginian who would later plague the English himself. His name was George Washington.

"Father, I cannot tell a lie: I cut down the cherry tree." An 1889 engraving by John C. McRae depicts an apocryphal event held dear by generations of Americans. *Library of Virginia, Richmond.* Below: Woodcut of tobacco (*Nicotiana tabacum*) with the oldest printed picture of a cigar smoker, from *Stirpium adversaria nova* by Lobelius, 1576. *The Granger Collection*

"*I have a large family of my own,* and my doors are open to Every Body, yet I have no Bills to pay, and half-a-Crown will rest undisturbed in my Pocket for many Moons Together. Like one of the Patriarchs, I have my Flocks and my Herds, my Bond-men and Bond-women, and every Soart of Trade amongst my own Servants, so that I live in a kind of Independence on every one but Providence."

Colonial planter William Byrd II of Westover Plantation, letter to a friend in England, c. 1733. Byrd was an early and colorful member of the Virginia dynasty whose most influential scion was Senator and Governor Harry Byrd (1887–1966).

George Washington and General Rochambeau Calling on Cornwallis at Nelson House, Yorktown by Edward L. Henry, 1873. In October 1781, the forces of Lord Cornwallis surrendered to Washington at Yorktown, effectively ending the Revolutionary War. *Virginia Museum of Fine Arts, Richmond*

Breaking with Britain

Although the English won the French and Indian War, their problems in the American colonies were far from over. The Stamp Act and other new taxes in the 1760s alienated the colonists, and firebrands like Virginia's Patrick Henry railed against British tyranny. By 1774 a Continental Congress had been convened in Philadelphia, and Virginians were among its most vocal representatives. When hostilities broke out, Continental forces came under the leadership of Virginia's George Washington—and a compatriot, Thomas Jefferson, penned a Declaration of Independence, signed by members of the Second Continental Congress.

As the new country struggled to define itself, Virginians again played a key role, contributing four of the first five presidents—Washington, Jefferson, James Madison, and James Monroe. During Washington's tenure, the newly planned federal capital—which encompassed part of the old northern Virginia port of Alexandria—began to rise on the banks of the Potomac.

"THE WAR IS ACTUALLY BEGUN! THE NEXT GALE THAT SWEEPS from the North will bring to our ears the clash of resounding arms! Our Brethren are already in the field! Why stand we here idle?…Is life so dear, or peace so sweet as to be purchased at the price of chains and slavery? Forbid it, Almighty God! I know not what course others may take, but as for me, give me liberty, or give me death!"

Patrick Henry, speech to members of the Virginia Convention, March 1775

Patrick Henry makes his famous speech to the Virginia House of Burgesses in 1774. *Library of Virginia, Richmond. Opposite:* Indian peace medal, 1776. *British Museum, London*

Right: Drummer Boy by Julian Scott, 1891. David David Gallery, Philadelphia. Photo Superstock
Below: A 19th-century weathervane of painted sheet metal depicts Civil War soldiers. Christie's Images

$\mathbf{B}$y the mid-19th century, the industrialized northern states and the agricultural southern ones were at odds over slavery and many other issues. Virginia sat squarely between the two factions, both politically and geographically. In 1859, Kansas abolitionist John Brown targeted the federal arsenal at Harpers Ferry for his historic raid.

When southern cotton states, strongly reliant on slavery, began seceding after Lincoln's election, Virginia and her pro-Union governor, John Letcher, tried unsuccessfully to negotiate a compromise between North and South. Although slavery did not fuel Virginia's economy, a strong sense of states' rights prevailed, and when Lincoln called for Virginia volunteers to fight the breakaway states, the Old Dominion quickly sided with her Dixie sisters. ❀

"WITH A SAD HEAVY HEART, MY DEAR CHILD, I WRITE, FOR THE prospects before us are sad indeed & as I think both parties are wrong in this fratricidal war, there is nothing comforting even in the hope that God may prosper the right, for I see no right in the matter. We can only pray that in his mercy he will spare us."

Mary Custis Lee, wife of Robert E. Lee, in a letter to her daughter Mildred, April 20, 1861

The Monitor and the Merrimack—the First Fight Between Ironclads by J. O. Davidson for L. Prang & Co., Boston, c. 1886. *The Library of Virginia, Richmond/Superstock* In March 1862, the CSS *Virginia*, renamed after its conversion to an ironclad, attacked federal wooden warships in Hampton Roads, destroying two of them; the next day, the *Monitor* fought her to a draw.

The Road to Appomattox

Powerhouse of the Confederacy, the Old Dominion had an industrial output almost equal to that of all the other southern states combined. Tredegar Iron Works, in Richmond, armed the South, and the state's coal and iron mines and railroads were vital to the war effort. But Virginia's geographic situation cost her dear. For four years the land was bathed in blood, as the forces of Robert E. Lee and an ever-changing host of northern commanders fought back and forth between Washington and Richmond. Besides losing countless men, Virginia also lost her western half when citizens on the far side of the Alleghenies voted to secede and form a new state—West Virginia.

Above: Lee in Richmond by Matthew Brady, 1865. The persistent photographer tracked Lee down just after the surrender. *Library of Congress. Right: The Old Westover Mansion* by Edward Lamson Henry, 1869. *Corcoran Gallery of Art, Washington, D.C.* Reconstruction did not deal kindly with Virginia, which remained economically depressed for decades. *Opposite: Winter Quarters, Culpeper, Virginia* by D. James, 1864. Union troops encamped in Culpeper in 1863. *Virginia Museum of Fine Arts, Richmond*

Army of Northern Virginia, fabulous army,
Strange army of ragged individualists,
The hunters, the riders, the walkers, the savage pastorals...
Army of planters' sons and rusty poor-whites...
                              Praying army,
Full of revivals, as full of salty jests,...
Army of improvisators of peanut-coffee
Who baked your bread on a ramrod stuck through the dough,
Swore and laughed and despaired and sang "Lorena,"
Suffered, died, deserted, fought to the end....

Stephen Vincent Benét, from "John Brown's Body," 1928

The Great Battles
In all, some 2,150 engagements took place on Virginia soil, including First and Second Manassas (1861, 1862), Fredericksburg (1862), Chancellorsville (1863), the Wilderness, Spotsylvania, Cold Harbor (1864), and the final siege of Petersburg (1864-65). Most of these sites are now protected as national battlefield parks.

> *"[T]he life of a Husbandman of all others*
> is the most delectable. It is honorable. It is amusing, and,
> with judicious management, it is profitable."
>
> *George Washington, in a letter to Alexander Spotswood, 1788*

Steeles Tavern by N. C. Wyeth, c. 1920s. Courtesy American Harvester Photo Corbis-Bettmann

"Fruitfullest Virginia"

Although legend pictures colonial Virginians as lords of vast plantations, in fact most worked small family plots of land with few or no slaves. That tradition of family farms continued into this century. The state's greatest contribution to agriculture came from the Shenandoah Valley, where in 1831 a 22-year-old named Cyrus McCormick introduced his reaper. While rural Virginia still looks quaintly agricultural, few of its remaining commercial farms are family affairs today; small-scale agribusiness has taken over the vegetable farms of the Eastern Shore, the hog and poultry husbandry of the central Shenandoah, and the grain fields of the Piedmont.

The End of the Hunt. Anonymous folk painting, c. 1800. *The Granger Collection, New York* Below: The McCormick Farm, near Raphine in the Shenandoah Valley. Now popular with visitors, this was the home of Cyrus McCormick, who first demonstrated his revolutionary reaper at nearby Steeles Tavern. The big millwheel is still turning, and one can see the log workshop where young Cyrus tinkered. *Photo Pat and Chuck Blackley*

In the area south of the James called Southside, peanuts and hog farming have held their own. Peanuts—fried, roasted, and in the shell—and Smithfield hams are cherished Virginia comestibles. Cotton still whitens some fields, though cotton was never king here, and the boom days of textile production have long since passed. But family orchardists still harvest summer peaches and an abundance of fall apples. And horse farms remain a passion of the well-heeled gentry.

"THOSE HORSEY PEOPLE, THEY WANT JUST THE RIGHT MIX of feed for their horses, and they'll pay anything. Why, they'd stick dollar bills in a horse's mouth, if they thought he'd eat it."

Velma Terry, Piedmont alfalfa grower, 1992

Harvesting the Sea

Marine biologists hail Chesapeake Bay as the country's most productive spawning ground for saltwater fish. But the area's traditional watermen didn't need scientists to tell them that, as they have long harvested its bounty of bluefish, spot, and flounder. The bay's shellfish are legion: oysters, clams, and, most abundantly, the "beautiful swimmers"—the blue crabs that rank as the region's chief delicacy. Some bay denizens— oysters and sea bass (locally known as rockfish)—have suffered from blight and the effects of pollution. But efforts to save the bay have paid off, and the creatures prized as seafood are returning—though not with them the legendary Chesapeake watermen. Only a handful of these weather-toughened men work the bay waters today, and their big-sailed skipjacks have virtually disappeared. One relict community survives on Tangier Island, in the middle of the bay, where families still harvest the Chesapeake and speak with the distinctive Devon and Cornish intonations of their ancestors.

"Blue crabs are not awe-inspiring like whales, formidable like sharks, splendid like marlins, or near-humanly lovable like porpoises. They are small, quick, alert, aggressive—yet endearing all the same in their feistiness, their readiness for unequal combat with their captor."

Novelist John Barth, in his introduction to
Beautiful Swimmers by William W. Warner, 1987

Watermen on the Eastern Shore of Virginia Dig Clams with Their Feet by A. Aubrey Bodine, 1948. Bodine was a photographer for the *Baltimore Sun* from 1927 to 1970, and the newspaper's Sunday rotogravure magazine became a showcase for his talent. Many of his richly toned images of Chesapeake Bay scenes were exhibited in museums, galleries, and photographic salons around the country. One of them inspired a 1975 poem by David Smith published in the *New Yorker,* which included the line, "… a little dream composing a little water…" *Bodine Collection, The Mariners' Museum, Newport News*

View of the busy waters of the Elizabeth River and Hampton Roads, where naval and commercial ships have ported since colonial times. Norfolk is on the left, Portsmouth on the right. Color lithograph by E. Sachse, 1851. *The Mariners' Museum, Newport News*

During World War II, Uncle Sam dragged Virginia from the clutches of her rural past and into the industrial 20th century. The Hampton Roads area became a hotbed of military-industrial might, fueled by two of the largest such complexes in the world: the Norfolk Naval Base, home port for some 150 vessels; and the Newport News shipyard, founded by robber baron Collis Huntington. It produced behemoth *Nimitz*-class aircraft carriers, other Navy ships, and the luxury liner SS *United States*. The NASA complex in neighboring Hampton was the training site for the first astronauts. Nearby Fort Monroe, a pivotal Union inholding during the Civil War, still retains its dignified, moated presence at the tip of Old Point Comfort.

In northern Virginia, the immense Pentagon, built in a record-breaking 16 months, sprawls over Arlington County's Potomac shoreline and overlooks the nation's capital. This Defense Department nerve center along with other federal agencies drives much of the area's economy. But the ride can be bumpy, dependent as it is on the budget-contracting or -expanding moods of Congress. ❧

The palm, and the pine, and the sea sands brown;
The far sea songs of the pleasure crews;
The air like balm in this building town—
And that is the picture of Newport News.

Joaquin Miller, "Newport News," c. 1897

Above: NASA rocket launch in Hampton. It was at this NASA facility that the Mercury astronauts trained for America's first manned space missions. *Photo Michael R. Brown. Left:* Aerial view of the Pentagon in Arlington. *Photo Cameron Davidson/Folio, Inc.*

The Business of History

In the 1920s, an Episcopal reverend in the Tidewater managed to interest John D. Rockefeller, Jr., in the dilapidated homes of a little village called Williamsburg. Since then, Colonial Williamsburg, a private foundation, has grown into one of the world's most acclaimed and lucrative historic re-creations. Welcoming more than a million visitors a year, the 173-acre complex, with its 88 original colonial buildings and hundreds of replicas, has given rise to a raft of surrounding tourist attractions, from the Busch Gardens amusement complex to a string of outlet centers.

Williamsburg's success inspired the state and federal government to exploit the historic worth of nearby Jamestown

Above: "I teach Bowling" from *The Marvelous Diary of Captain John Smith.* The "diary" was a clever promotional item printed by the Hotel Chamberlain in Old Point Comfort, c. early 1900s. Purporting to be Smith's diary, discovered in a room at the inn, it depicted him as a time traveler in such anachronistic pursuits as bowling, quaffing cocktails in the lobby, and observing modern ships in Hampton Roads. *Private collection. Right:* A colonial garden re-created at Jamestown. *Virginia Tourism Corp.*

Horse-drawn carriage in Colonial Williamsburg. The village of costumed interpreters convincingly dramatize daily life in Virginia's colonial capital on the eve of revolution. *Photo Scott Barrow*

Island, part of the national park system; the state's re-created Jamestown Settlement; and the Yorktown Battlefield, where the world of British colonial rule was turned upside down. Outside this so-called Colonial Triangle are countless other historic homes that draw visitors—from Washington's Mount Vernon, on the banks of the Potomac, to Stratford Hall, the family seat of the Lees (Richard Henry, Robert E., and their kin), and westward to Belle Grove in the Shenandoah Valley, a classic columned manor that once quartered Union troops and is now a National Trust property.

Historical Highlights

Belle Grove
South of Winchester on Rte. 11
540-869-2028

Colonial National Historical Park
(Jamestown Island, Colonial Parkway, Yorktown Battlefield)
757-229-1733

Colonial Williamsburg
757-229-1000 or 800-HISTORY

George Washington's Mount Vernon Estate and Gardens
703-780-3383

Jamestown Settlement
757-253-4838

Montpelier
540-672-2728

Coal miners work by candlelight in a Cumberland area mine, 1939. Photographer unknown. Although the prosperity that coal brought to this part of Virginia was short-lived, this industry helped shape the region's rough-and-ready character. *Library of Virginia, Richmond*

In the late 19th century, it seemed as if the coalfields of southwestern Virginia might turn the area into an industrial powerhouse. But Virginia's soft coal proved unsatisfactory for steel-making and other heavy industry; though coal trucks still rumble through the Alleghenies, mining is a relatively minor concern.

Other kinds of manufacturing have prospered in Virginia, with food processing currently at the top of the list. Although they are not exactly food, tobacco products have long been a major industry in the Richmond area. Colonial Virginians were so convinced of the commercial worth of the "estimable weed" that they even planted it in the streets of Jamestown—but the Old Dominion ceased to be a major grower even before the colonial era was over, its soil depleted by the voracious crop. Still, cigarette makers like Liggett and Myers (Chesterfields), Lorillard (Old Golds), and the Reynolds Company (Camels) reigned in Richmond through the 1950s; the remaining tobacco titan is Philip Morris, now headquartered in a complex designed by architect Gordon Bunshaft. ❀

"A custome lothsome to the eye, hateful to the Nose, harmfull to the braine, daungerous to the Lungs, and in the black, stinking fume thereof, neerest resembling the horrible Stigian smoke of the pit that is bottomelesse."

England's King James I on smoking tobacco, 1620s

Above: Pocahontas tobacco label. *Left: A Liberated Woman* by John George Brown, advertising art for Virginia Slims cigarettes. *Christie's Images.* Some Virginia cigarette producers have stayed with their primary product despite public-health and government pressures. Reynolds, however, underwent a corporate transition from making cigarettes to making the foil liners for packs, with aluminum eventually becoming its chief product.

Above: The Moaners Bench by Julien Binford, c. 1941. Reynolds Gallery, Richmond. Opposite below: An old church in the Cumberland Gap region. Photo Ric Ergenbright

In colonial Virginia, white citizens were required to attend church once a month—and church meant the Anglican variety. This law created a string of small, elegant brick churches scattered through the Tidewater, many of which still function as Episcopal parishes. With independence from England came, presumably, religious freedom. But in Virginia the fact that a man or woman—black or white, rich or poor—was a "good churchgoer" conferred a definite social status. In the black community the church was an important social and political force, a place where parishioners could claim their voices in ways otherwise prohibited. Those voices, among other things, gave rise to a rich tradition of gospel music. Even today, the white steeples of Baptist and Methodist churches rise above small towns, and in Virginia Beach, televangelist Pat Robertson guides the faithful from his Christian Broadcasting Center. A quieter version of the old-time religion prevails among the Protestant churches of the Shenandoah Valley.✿

Scotch-Irish settlers ventured into western Virginia in the 18th century and founded Protestant churches, as did German Mennonites, who still travel by horse and buggy and tend their fields as they have for a century.
Photo Everett Johnson

"SHENANDOAH TOWNS WERE NOTED FOR THREE THINGS. Churches, academies of learning, and distilleries. The latter flourished in spite of the former, and among a less sturdy, intelligent and godly race of people, would have led to utter demoralization."

Rev. William S. White, D.D., and His Times: An Autobiography, *1891*

Water Wonders

The harbors and bays that feather the Virginia coast are both a blessing and a curse. Historically, a system of lighthouses has warned mariners of shoally waters and unseen spits, and some of those nostalgically blinking beacons still stand. At Old Point Comfort, a stone tower erected in 1802 monitors the entrance to Hampton Roads. The candy-striped Assateague Lighthouse that once overlooked the Atlantic now sits inland, thanks to shifting currents and beach build-up. Cape Henry, where the Chesapeake Bay and the Atlantic meet, boasts two beachside lights: the buff-colored Old Cape Henry Lighthouse, commissioned by George Washington, ranks as the oldest government-built light in the country; the

"new" lighthouse that replaced it has itself stood since 1881.

Help of a different kind was needed for land traffic to negotiate the coastal filigree of waters, so Virginians became bridge builders. Their efforts peaked in the early 1960s with the building of a 17.6-mile-long bridge–tunnel across the bay, linking the southern Eastern Shore to the mainland at last. Leapfrogging across four manmade islands, the span includes two mile-long tunnels, two bridges, two miles of causeway, and 12 miles of trestled roadway. The complex now bears the name of its mastermind designer, Lucius J. Kellam, Jr.

Dismal Swamp Canal by Robert W. Salmon, 1830. George Washington envisioned this canal and many others. He dreamed of linking the East Coast to the Rocky Mountains via a system of canals. This one opened in 1805, after his death. *Virginia Museum of Fine Arts, Richmond*

Virginia pine overlooks the Shenandoah Valley, near Skyline Drive. Travelers can catch glimpses of the river's many bends from roadside viewpoints.
Photo Carr Clifton/ Minden Pictures

Thanks to FDR and his 1930s WPA projects, the crest of the Blue Ridge is lined by two of the loveliest road systems in the country. The 105-mile-long Skyline Drive follows the northern end of the ridge from Front Royal to Rockfish Gap, offering long views down on the Shenandoah River and valley and the hollows once peopled by hardscrabble mountain families. (Admittedly, the road system and the ensuing Shenandoah National Park sounded a death knell for the mountain folks' already waning lifestyle.) Even more ambitious in conception is the contiguous Blue Ridge Parkway, which picks up where the Skyline Drive ends, continuing another 469 miles south through Virginia and into North Carolina. Along the way, it passes the ridge's low point, at 649 feet, where the James River breaches the mountains. A restored canal lock here is a reminder of the unsuccessful 19th-century James River and Kanawha Canal, designed to link the fertile western lands with the coast. 🏵

Summer in the Blue Ridge by Hugh Bolton Jones, 1874. Until the national park was established in the 1930s, small farms were scattered all through this mountainous backcountry; today, travelers on the Blue Ridge Parkway can visit a re-created mountain farmstead in the park. *Christie's Images*

Confederate President Jefferson Davis surveys Richmond's Monument Avenue from the top of his memorial, designed by Edward Valentine, 1907. The avenue's statuary now culminates in the west with a monument to local son and tennis great Arthur Ashe. *Photo Richard T. Nowitz/Corbis*

Heroes and Battlefields

Locate the courthouse in almost any Virginia town and nearby will stand a statue of a Confederate soldier, still guarding it as if the war never ended. And somewhere in the nearby countryside may be an old battlefield and a cemetery filled with Civil War dead. These days, passion for a cause lost almost 150 years ago is waning, but the stone memorials remain. What is probably the proudest array of Confederate heroes anywhere can be found on Richmond's Monument Avenue, a broad boulevard graced by massive likenesses of Jefferson Davis, Robert E. Lee, Jeb Stuart, Stonewall Jackson—and, incongruously, Matthew Fontaine Maury, the early charter of Atlantic currents.

Richmond also supports a large, wooded Victorian cemetery—Hollywood—where one pyramidal marker honors the mass grave of hundreds of Confederates. Their president, Jefferson Davis, is buried here, too, as are U.S. presidents James Monroe and John Tyler. Encircling the city are thousands of acres of battlefield, reminders of battles fought early and late in the conflict. War also haunts the landscape around Fredericksburg, Manassas, and throughout the Shenandoah Valley.

The Civil War gave the nation its official military graveyard: Arlington National Cemetery. During the war, the U.S. Army's quartermaster confiscated the Arlington home of Robert E. Lee's family and began burying Union dead on the grounds.

Today the cemetery sprawls across 612 hilly acres above the Potomac, its ranks of simple white headstones marching to within sight of the Pentagon.

Left: Stonewall Jackson strikes a heroic equestrian pose. In reality, the great general sat his horse, Little Sorrel, less than gracefully, but the artist is permitted his vision. *Photo Richard T. Nowitz/Corbis. Above:* Stained-glass mural by Ami Shamir, 1970, memorial to the Virginia cadets killed in the battle of New Market. *Hall of Valor, Civil War Museum, New Market. Photo Catherine Karnow/Woodfin Camp & Associates*

Ironically, it was the liberal Thomas Jefferson who most influenced the tenor of Virginia's conservative politics. Jefferson's advocacy of states' rights and his idyllic view of an agrarian life, based on local concerns of farm and family, inspired Virginians—and many other southerners—to secede from the Union in pursuit of their own, more local notions of government.

States' rights and a stubborn provincialism remained the rallying points behind Virginia politics through the first half of the 20th century. From the mid-1920s through the 40s, the Byrd Machine—which writer John Gunther called "the most urbane and genteel dictatorship in America"—thrived under the strong arm of Senator Harry Byrd, controlling state politics and even, to some extent, state mores. Discriminatory Jim Crow laws were taken for granted by white Virginians well into the 1950s, and when the federal government announced desegregation, Virginia launched a strident, if brief, opposition. Ever unpredictable, however, the state elected the nation's first African-American governor, Douglas Wilder, some 40 years later. ❀

"THE ONLY SANE AND CONSTRUCTIVE COURSE TO follow is to remain in the house of our fathers— even though the roof leaks, and there be bats in the belfry, rats in the pantry, a cockroach waltz in the kitchen and skunks in the parlor."

Governor J. Lindsay Almond in a speech at Norfolk, 1948

Nat Turner and fellow escaped slaves in Tidewater swampland. In 1831, Turner and his followers rebelled and killed about 50 whites—the largest violent uprising of slaves in U.S. history. Color engraving, c. late 1800s. *The Granger Collection. Opposite above:* **Governor Douglas Wilder** *Opposite below:* **Senator Harry Byrd and his family.** *Both, Library of Virginia, Richmond*

> *"Architecture is my delight. And putting up and pulling down one of my favorite amusements."*
>
> Thomas Jefferson

One of the few true Renaissance men to emerge from colonial America, Thomas Jefferson had a passion for many things—fine wine, horticulture, music, almost anything French, and architecture. While his other passions survive only in his writing, his love of neoclassical symmetry and domes still marks Virginia's built environment. The small, elegant state capitol is his creation, and he liberally lent his opinions to the lay-

out and design of the federal city and the President's House, as the White House was then known. On seeing his plans for adding onto the latter, Federal-era architect Benjamin Latrobe lamented Jefferson's "prejudices in favor of the old french [*sic*] books, out of which he fishes everything."

The American Institute of Architects does not share Latrobe's opinion of Jefferson's talents.

Above: Thomas Jefferson by Gilbert Stuart, 1805. National Portrait Gallery, Smithsonian Institution. Left: Jefferson's Cabinet, or study, was furnished with a whirligig chair and inventive writing equipment. *Photo Robert C. Lautman. Opposite: The University of Virginia (the Lawn). Photo Ted Hooper*

It proclaimed Jefferson's design of the colon-naded pavilions at the University of Virginia an outstanding achievement of American architecture, and UNESCO has designated them a World Heritage Site. Even more revealing of Jefferson's aesthetic sensibilities are his two private homes. Monticello, his famous jewel of both formality and ingenuity, actually tops a small mountain (a *monticello,* in Italian) near the university. Less well known but perhaps more compelling, the newly renovated Poplar Forest is the villa hideaway Jefferson designed for himself in Bedford County. ❀

Jefferson Designs

Monticello
Rte. 53, Charlottesville
804-984-9822

Poplar Forest
Rte. 661, Lynchburg
804-525-1806

University of Virginia
Charlottesville
804-924-0311

Capitol of Virginia
9th and Grace Sts., Richmond
804-786-4344

Above: Mount Vernon from the West, **attributed to Edward Savage, c. 1791.** *Christie's Images* **Opposite above: Footbridge in the garden of the Khan residence, Fredericksburg.** *Photo Pieter Estersohn. Opposite below:* **Silver goblet by Claude-Nicolas Delanoy, 1789, designed by Thomas Jefferson.**

Since the era of cavaliers and manorial plantations along the James River, Virginians have proudly cultivated the arts of living well. Perhaps nowhere else in the country do so many outstanding colonial and early 19th-century country residences survive—many of them embellished with original furnishings and decorative objects. Preserving the past—both its physical evidence and its traditions—has long been a hallowed cause here, saving many fine old structures and antiques from the march of progress. Towering, centuries-old allées of boxwood and oak have survived as well, thanks to that respect for the venerable and time-tested. The Mount Vernon Ladies Association, founded in 1853 to preserve George Washington's Potomac River estate, ranks as the country's first historic preservation society, working to safeguard, among other things, the property's sylvan views.

Virginians of all classes feel that their home is their castle. Decorative rather than fine arts have always characterized the state's tastes; fine

moldings, graceful staircases, brass candlesticks, handmade quilts, and heirloom tea sets polished to a high gloss are well-established standards of gentility. ✤

"I LIKE VIRGINIA, AND I LIKE VIRGINIANS. BECAUSE VIRGINIANS are all snobs, and I like snobs. A snob has to spend so much time being a snob that he has little left to meddle with you, and so it is very pleasant."

William Faulkner during his tenure as writer-in-residence at the University of Virginia

At Home in the Country

Virginia's country estates are legendary, anchored by imposing Georgian homes amid green fields where long-legged thoroughbreds graze. The prototype of this picture is Albemarle County in the Piedmont—Jefferson's homeland—where lately many of the wealthy and celebrated have acquired homes: industrialist John Kluge; actors Jessica Lange, Sam Shepard, and Sissy Spacek; and writers Rita Mae Brown and Ann Beattie, among others. But the Virginia country house reaches its true glory in the colonial plantations that still reign on sloping river bluffs above the James. Great homes like Westover, Berkeley, and Shirley (the oldest working plantation in the country) exemplify the center-hall stateliness of colonial

design. Even "nouveau" country homes around the state strive for antebellum grace with columns and fanlights.

Early in this century, as preservation became a passion, the Colonial Revival style swept through the Tidewater, adding a more livable, elegant gloss to the barebones, uncarpeted authenticity of orthodox colonial decor. An exemplar of that period, Williamsburg's Carter's Grove, sublimely unites 20th-century taste and money with a colonial edifice.

Above: Interior of the Khan residence, Fredericksburg. This early 19th-century plantation house was redecorated in 1997 by jewelry designer Kenneth Jay Lane. *Photo Pieter Estersohn. Right:* Pope–Leighey House, Fairfax County, by Frank Lloyd Wright, 1941. One of Wright's Usonian homes, this was built for journalist Loren Pope and later moved to its current location on the grounds of Woodlawn Plantation. *Photo John Skowronski. Opposite above:* The dining room at Gunston Hall, Fairfax County. Its woodwork was the work of William Buckland, who came to Virginia as an indentured servant but became a renowned woodworker and later a gentleman architect. *Photo John Skowronski Opposite below:* Chatham Manor, Fredericksburg. *Photo Patricia Lanza*

At Home in Town

The burgeoning colonial economy of Virginia soon gave rise to a well-to-do merchant class, and these early businessmen

settled themselves in growing port towns like Norfolk, Portsmouth, and Alexandria. Like the landed country barons, they too favored the Georgian style, building stately town-houses with imposing center halls and fanlit doorways. Decorative brass and porcelain, ornate fireplace surrounds and woodwork, and impressive entry halls characterized the town homes, just as they had the country estates.

The Federal period continued the love affair with Georgian symmetry, though the lines and decor were simpler and more refined. In the 19th century, a crowd of Victorian townhouses rose on the streets of Richmond and Alexandria—the last hurrah of a passing era before brick ramblers and neighborhood developments re-created pseudo-country in the suburbs.

Above: The imposing Georgian facade of Carlyle House in Alexandria. John Carlyle, who built it in 1753, was a Scottish merchant who married into the Fairfaxes, one of Virginia's best families. *Photo Rick Buettner/Folio, Inc. Left: Mrs. Seth Wilkinson.* Artist unknown, c. 1825–30. *Abby Aldrich Rockefeller Folk Art Center, Colonial Williamsburg. Opposite above:* Victorian row houses in a Richmond residential neighborhood. *Photo Jeff Greenberg/ Rainbow. Opposite below:* Wickham House in Richmond, built in 1812, is a showcase of early 19th-century Federal style, including this delicate woodwork. *Valentine Museum*

During the Evening by Charles Dana Gibson, 1899. *Private collection* Opposite above: Tureen, c. 1786, from George and Martha Washington's dinner service. *Winterthur Museum* Opposite below: Quilt in a stylized house-and-tree pattern, probably made by an African-American woman, c. 1900. *America Hurrah Archive, New York*

Virginians have elevated their long tradition of hospitality to an art form, graciously entertaining even their enemies with food, drink, and polite conversation. In fact, the obligation to extend universal hospitality plagued two Virginia presidents, Washington and Jefferson, who were obliged to feed and quarter the perpetual round of strangers who came to pay their respects.

Traditionally, the lady of the house saw to the proper entertaining of guests, and the state has produced an impressive legacy of fine hostesses. Entertaining in style is a badge of honor, and hostesses proudly bring out their family china, silver, and linen, their pewter Jefferson cups, and their favored family recipes. Fine needlework, too, has been a tradition since George Washington's step-granddaughter, Nelly Custis, created intricate needlepoint at her Woodlawn estate.

The appeal of a Virginia woman, with her charm and innate elegance, became a national standard when turn-of-the-century artist Charles Dana Gibson used his Virginia-born wife, Irene Langhorne (whose sister was Lady Nancy Astor), as the prototype for his willowy Gibson Girls. If the southern belle is by now an anachronism, her attention to social graces remains part and parcel of Virginia's love affair with the past.✿

"THE GENTRY OF VIRGINIA dwelt on their great lands after a fashion almost patriarchal.... Their hospitality was boundless. No stranger was ever sent away from their gates. The gentry received one another, and travelled to each other's houses, in a state almost feudal."

William Makepeace Thackeray,
The Virginians, *1911*

Eating Well, Virginia Style

Virginians endeavor to make any meal, whether formal or casual, a festive occasion, and their culinary traditions reflect their hospitable largesse. Intense, salty Smithfield ham (raised and cured only in Smithfield) is the state's signature delicacy, sliced thin and often stuffed into flaky beaten biscuits. Fried chicken, deviled crabs, scalloped oysters, and slow-cooked barbecue are other longstanding favorites—washed down with generously sweetened iced tea or bourbon. The latter may be served simply as bourbon and "branch" (an old reference to branch water) or on summer days in mint juleps. Dinner may end with classic southern desserts like pecan or mincemeat pie.

Al fresco festivities are popular. In summer, groups gather for crab fests, cooking the delicacies in their shells, then digging in with both hands to pick out the

Above: Williamsburg epergne with fruit and dessert. *Kelly/Mooney Photography. Right:* Label for a brand of Smithfield ham. *Collection Peter D. Pruden, III. Opposite above:* Pineapple roof ornament at Brandon Plantation. *Opposite below:* Mint julep. *Both photos, William Strode*

Regina's Virginia Bourbon Cake

This family recipe may fall back on the expedient of boxed cake and pudding mixes, but there is nothing "canned" about its powerful bourbon punch. Note: it should be baked the day before you plan to serve it.

½ cup water
½ cup vegetable oil
½ cup sugar
½ cup bourbon
4 large eggs
1 box instant vanilla pudding
1 box moist cake mix
1 cup chopped walnuts

Preheat oven to 350° F. Combine all ingredients, except walnuts, and beat for 4 minutes. Pour into a greased and floured tube pan lined with the walnuts and bake 1 hour. Cool in the pan.

Bourbon Sauce
1 stick butter
½ cup sugar
½ cup your best bourbon

Melt to boiling and simmer gently until sugar is completely dissolved. Gently puncture holes in top of cake, still in pan, and pour half of the bourbon sauce over the cake. Invert the cake onto a serving platter and pour the remaining sauce on top. Cover with foil and let season at least 12 hours before serving.

succulent meat and dip it in drawn butter. In the fall, outdoor pig, oyster, and clam roasts usher in cooler weather, the oysters and clams roasted on an open fire till barely open and chased with "stone fences"— fresh apple cider spiked with bourbon. Holiday time brings its own traditions: eggnog frothing in punch bowls and tables adorned with pineapple centerpieces—the ancient fertility symbol became a decorative theme in 17th-century England and made its way into Virginia culture as a symbol of welcome.

A BLOOMING FEAST

Since their colonial forebears planted formal parterres and terraces, Virginians have appreciated and cultivated fine gardens. They take advantage of their land's natural profusion—particularly its spectacular spring displays of flowering trees. In late March and April, newly green woodlands are dashed with redbuds and the white lace of dogwoods; azaleas and rhododendron provide bolder color. The blooming bounty is celebrated by garden clubs, rose societies, and year-round festivals—dogwood, azalea, apple blossom. The biggest splash is Garden Week, when historic and contemporary homes and gardens throughout the state are open to the public.

Public gardens, too, are scattered throughout Virginia, from the Tidewater to the Blue Ridge. Many are attached to historic homes; notable among these are Monticello's authentic Jeffersonian garden, Maymont's superbly romantic European gardens, and Oatlands' Italianate splendor. A few stellar horticultural resources—the Norfolk Botanical Garden and Richmond's Louis Ginter Gardens—stand alone. But as dear to a Virginian's heart as any showy rose is the family vegetable patch—a few rows of corn, tomatoes, and peas that celebrate the earthy smells and sweet flavors of summer.

"*I watered your flowers this morning,*
and hoed another row of turnips, and expect to hill
some celery this evening. Your old man at home is tak-
ing good care of one somebody's flower-slips…hope
that little somebody is feeling lively as a lark!"

Major Thomas (Stonewall) Jackson to his wife, Anna,
September 15, 1859

Rose arbor at Chatham, near
Fredericksburg. Ellen Biddle
Shipman redesigned these gar-
dens in 1924. Hand-tinted
lantern slide. *Archives of American
Gardens, Smithsonian Institution
Opposite above:* The Louis Ginter
Gardens during tulip bloom.
*Photo Ted Hooper/Folio, Inc.
Opposite below:* T. Wood seed
catalog cover, 1907, boasts an
image of Virginia's capitol.

Recreation is pursued with passion in Virginia, its form varying with location and season. In summer, with hundreds of miles of rivers, creeks, and bays at their disposal, Virginians take to the water. Powerboats towing intrepid water-skiers weave in and out among sailboats, and fishers vie for favorite spots "where the trout or spot are running." At summer's end, as the mountains and Piedmont turn tawny and crimson, hunters, hikers, and leaf-peepers take to the hills, and the fox-hunting set dons its riding pinks and begins the fall round of hunts and point-to-point races through the burnished countryside.

This is the season, too, for team sports, and stadiums fill with fans. Surprisingly for a sports-loving state, Virginia has few professional teams, but that may be because it is so focused on school athletics. In the dozens of colleges that sprinkle the Piedmont and Shenandoah, loyal alumni turn out in

The Hunt by Wallace Nall, 1978. Riding to hounds was one of the English civilities Virginia's early cavaliers imported to the New World. Well-heeled Virginians still practice the sport in the state's rolling horse country. In Albemarle County, an annual blessing of the hounds takes place at Thanksgiving time. *Courtesy the artist*

droves for football and basketball season, and even high school teams attract intense attention. That same sense of team spirit, infused with veneration for the past, may also inspire the reenactment aficionados: the hundreds of buffs who collect periodically on battlefields to recreate the glories and miseries of both the Revolutionary and Civil Wars. ❋

Midway (Small-Town Fair) by Kathryn Marie McNulty, c. 1950, depicts the Tazewell County Fair. Especially in rural western Virginia, such old-fashioned pastimes endure. *The Ogden Museum of Southern Art, New Orleans*

From William Byrd's colonial diaries to Civil War memoirs to 20th-century fiction, the Old Dominion has produced a long line of practitioners of the well-turned phrase. Among literary luminaries, native son Edgar Allan Poe, raised in Richmond and critic of its *Southern Literary Messenger,* looms large, as does post-bellum novelist Ellen Glasgow, who wrote revealingly of Virginia society. In his Pulitzer Prize–winning *Growing Up,* Russell Baker poignantly recalls his Depression-era boyhood in the Winchester area, where novelist Willa Cather was also born.

Since mid-century, when William Faulkner did a stint as writer-in-residence at the University of Virginia, Charlottesville has been the state's literary hub. Past and present residents of the area

include novelist and short-story craftsman Peter Taylor; poet Charles Wright; novelist Rita Mae Brown; and thriller scribe John Grisham. Patricia Cornwell, a former Richmond coroner, pens gritty bestsellers on (mostly) serial murders. Probably Virginia's most distinguished literary native of this century is William Styron, raised in Newport News. Styron distilled poignant, distinctly Virginia tragedies into his famous novels *The Confessions of Nat Turner* and *Lie Down in Darkness*—both set against the sultry backdrop of his native Tidewater. ❀

"I ROSE ABOUT 6, READ HEBREW AND GREEK. I PRAYED AND had hominy. The weather was cold and clear, the wind southwest....I read records and Latin till dinner when I ate sparerib. At night talked with my people. Mrs. Byrd had the headache pretty much. I prayed."

William Byrd, Secret Diary, *1740*

"I RAN DOWN A SYCAMORE-LINED STREET...RUNNING IN THE windless heat until the heat itself, thick as fur, slowed me to a listless walk. The village was coming awake. Those sentinel radios had begun to blare from the open windows. I heard hallelujahs as some evangelist got down to work. The air was starting to bloom with the Sabbath's twitter and cacophony ... As they did every Sunday, Flying Fortresses in formation from the Army airfield droned low over the village, the engines a massed mutter at first, then swelling into a racket that hurt the eardrums, deafened. I stopped and stood still, peering upward through the shadows cast by the wings, waiting for the flight to pass."

William Styron, from his short story "A Tidewater Morning," 1987

A performance of *Stonewall Country* at the Lime Kiln Theatre in Lexington. As well as this perennial production, the company presents other plays in its picturesque outdoor setting—the remains of an old lime kiln with thick stone walls and an earth floor. *Courtesy Lime Kiln Theatre.* Below: The Barter Theatre in Abingdon, c. 1970s. Over the years, this outstanding small theater has drawn playgoers from every continent. *Photo State Theatre of Virginia*

Tickets for Peanuts

America's very first theater was built on the east side of Williamsburg's Palace Green sometime between 1716 and 1718, by dance master William Levingston. No one knows what kind of productions were staged, and in 1745 the building was converted to a courtroom. Richmond had a proper theater by about 1800, but it was destroyed in 1811 by the first of the nation's many devastating theater fires in the 19th century.

An official state theater got its start in the Depression, when a hungry young actor decided that if he moved back to his native Virginia from New York, he might be able to eat and act both. Robert Porterfield's Barter Theatre in Abingdon charged admission in the form of produce; locals could see a play in exchange for their hams and jams, or for labor ("vittles or work"). More than just a curiosity, the theater became a rousing success, and such notables as Tennessee Williams and Noel Coward accepted "in-kind" payment for their playwriting. As the State Theatre of Virginia, the company still offers plays in repertory at two theaters for those who find their way to far-western Abingdon.

Historical reenactment dramas have long been popular in this state that loves its history; the best of these is easily the acclaimed Lime Kiln Theatre productions of *Stonewall Country* in Lexington.

"SUPPOSE I BRING IN A TURKEY WORTH FOUR DOLLARS. Do you give me ten pounds of string beans and a rabbit in change? Or does your cashier chew off thirty-five cents worth of white meat?"

Radio comedian Fred Allen on his syndicated radio show, to Robert Porterfield, founder of the Barter Theatre, c. 1930s

The stars of television's *The X-Files* on one of their missions. *Photofest*

Reel-Life Virginia

Some 30 box-office films were shot in Virginia in the 1990s, including *The Jackal, G.I. Jane, Deep Impact,* and *The People vs. Larry Flynt.* With its proximity to the nation's capital and the CIA's Langley headquarters, Virginia's countryside is often the background for films involving government intrigue, including *The Pelican Brief* and *True Lies.* And TV's dynamic *X-Files* duo often find themselves weaving down foggy, forest-draped Virginia lanes on the trail of aliens. More experimental fare shows up at Charlottes-ville's annual October film festival.

Musical Traditions

For centuries, Virginia's black musicians have been singing their souls out. The Piedmont blues tradition got its start among field workers, and though it's hard to find these days, a talented few still twang out this distinctive brand of the blues. By mid-century, clubs and dance halls in Richmond and the Tidewater were rich with such local talent as Pearl Bailey, Ella Fitzgerald, and Bill "Bojangles" Robinson. Country music, too, has deep roots in western Virginia. Vocalists Patsy Cline and Mother Maybelle Carter hailed from there, as did the Statler Brothers, who now have their own museum in Staunton. To the contemporary jazz and rock worlds, Virginia has contributed the influential jazz guitarist Charlie Byrd and sixties legend Jim Morrison. More recently, the Dave Matthews Band, a Charlottesville group, has made its mark on the pop charts.

Both popular and classical music concerts by world-class performers take place at Wolf Trap Farm Park for the Performing Arts in the northern Virginia suburbs, which claims to be "the only national park site dedicated solely to the performing arts." Richmond has its own symphony orchestra, and Norfolk's opera has been hailed as one of the nation's very best regional companies.

"RICHMOND WAS A JAZZ TOWN, TOO, WAS BUSY making its own jazz legends in speakeasies, dance halls, nip joints, hotel lobbies, ballrooms and clubs along Second Street, the early bastion of black business and social life."

Harriett McLeod, "2nd Street Jazz," in the
Richmond News Leader, *January 1985*

Above: Pearl Bailey. *Photo Herman Leonard/Stage-Image. Left:* Patsy Cline. Born in Winchester, Cline got her first big break by winning *Arthur Godfrey's Talent Scouts,* and her career peaked around 1960 with her biggest hit, "I Fall to Pieces." She died in a plane crash in 1963 but has influenced later female country vocalists. *Opposite above:* Musicians by Theresa Pollak, c. 1965. *Collection Mrs. Adele Stern. Opposite below:* A performance at Filene Center, Wolf Trap Foundation. *Photo Roger Foley/Folio, Inc.*

In Old Virginia, Belmont by Gari Melchers, c. 1918. *Belmont, The Gari Melchers Memorial Gallery and Mary Washington College, Fredericksburg*

Like all Virginians—and most artists—Virginia artists are an independent lot who have never clubbed together in a colony or school. In part this may be because patronage for serious art has been lacking, so creative souls have often left the state to establish themselves. Still, the Old Dominion can claim some fine talent. Nell

Blaine and Gari Melchers, a nonnative who spent his last years in Fredericksburg, produced romantic mid-century works in an Impressionist vein, while Jack Beal, Julien Binford, Anthony Watkins, and photographer Emmet Gowin have brought varying styles of realism to portraiture and landscape. More recently, two Virginians have captured the art world's attention: Sally Mann, whose photographs of her children and of southern scenes are hauntingly unforgettable; and Cy Twombly, whose best-known work interprets Greek myths through abstractions in line and color.

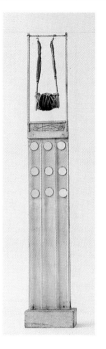

Above: Untitled by Cy Twombly, 1954. *Cy Twombly Gallery, The Menil Collection, Houston. Left: Living Room* by Philip Geiger, 1998. Geiger says that his subjects, the people and places of Charlottesville, "offer an endless opportunity to explore the interaction of light and place with human activity, relationship, and psychological mood." *Reynolds Gallery, Richmond*

Virginia Commonwealth University (formerly the Richmond School of Art) has been training new talent since 1928, when Theresa Pollak returned to the state after studying in New York, founded the school's art department, and went on to guide many young artists. A recent VCU graduate is Stephen Fox, whose moodily realistic landscapes are much acclaimed. Richmond's Reynolds Gallery is also a strong force for up-and-coming names like Fox and other in-state notables such as Ray Kass and Philip Geiger, both professors at Virginia universities. Richmond's Virginia Museum of Fine Arts, with its eclectic permanent collection, ranges far beyond any provincial vision; periodic special exhibits, called Un/Common Ground, feature Virginia artists with distinctive visions.

The art scene in Norfolk has lately burgeoned, thanks in large part to automobile mogul Walter Chrysler, whose superb collection of fine art and antiquities forms the core of the Chrysler Museum. In nearby Virginia Beach, the Contemporary Art Center of Virginia sponsors the popular Boardwalk Art Show each June. ✿

Above: George Washington by Anderson Johnson, c. 1985. Collection Ellin B. Gordon. Photo Tom Green. Left: Main Street, Tazewell, Virginia by Kathryn Marie McNulty, c. 1950. The artist first came to southwestern Virginia with her father, a civil engineer. She returned to Tazewell in the 1940s to open a studio and ceramic shop on Main Street—the setting for this and other paintings of daily rural life. *The Ogden Museum of Southern Art, New Orleans*

Imperial Russia Comes to Richmond

Lillian Thomas Pratt, a Virginia lady with a czarina's tastes, bequeathed her enameled, jewel-encrusted Easter eggs and bibelots to the Virginia Museum of Fine Arts in 1947. Today they rank as one of the paramount collections amassed in this country of works by Peter Carl Fabergé, jeweler to the last three Romanov czars. Before her death, the publicity-shy Mrs. Pratt summoned the museum's director to her home and sent him away with the staggering trove in the back of his station wagon.

Twentieth-Century Folk

One of the true gems of Colonial Williamsburg, tucked away amid the restored 18th-century town, the Busch Gardens theme park, the Governor's Palace, and countless other attractions, is the Abby Aldrich Rockefeller Folk Art Center.

Sweet Dreams, Swan Dreams

When Sally May Dooley, a turn-of-the-century Virginia grand dame, laid herself down to sleep, she was transported to dreamland on the back of this fanciful, larger-than-life swan. Her famous "swan bed," originally designed for the boudoir of her Blue Ridge Mountain villa, Swannanoa, today graces the bedroom of her former Richmond estate, Maymont.

Along with examples from past centuries, the center features some vivid works by self-taught artists of the 20th century. *Fish,* by Powhatan artist Robert Howell, was exhibited here in 1996.

Of Ships, Men, and Mosquitos

When you see the Jamestown Settlement's replicas of the three original colonist-bearing ships, you are struck by how small they are. The largest, the *Susan Constant,* weighs in at only 100 tons, the *Godspeed* only 40, and the *Discovery* a featherweight 20. Flimsy things, really, in which to cross an ocean, and they came packed with men—105 in all. They may also have carried a pest that plagues Virginians to this day: mosquitos, picked up in the tropics and thereby introduced to the continental New World.

Stalacpipe City

The "World's Largest Natural Musical Instrument," according to the 1988 *Guinness Book of Records,* is the Great Stalacpipe Organ, which sprawls over three acres in the Shenandoah Valley's Luray Caverns. Electronics engineer Leland Sprinkle came up with the idea of grinding and tuning the cave's stalactites to concert pitch, then outfitting them with rubber-tipped, electrically controlled plungers. Since its dedication in 1957, the organ has filled the caves with subterranean sonority and provided accompaniment for many weddings.

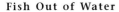

Fish Out of Water

In Virginia Beach, visitors strolling the historic boardwalk encounter several benefits of a recent renovation—such as a series of playful, larger-than-life sculptures of beach balls, hermit crabs, flying pelicans, a school of bluefish, and a sandcastle that won't wash away with the tide. Other attractions include the Old Coast Guard Station (dating from 1903) and the Atlantic Wildfowl Heritage Museum, housed in the last oceanfront cottage on the boardwalk.

Great People

A selective listing of native Virginians, concentrating on the arts.

Shirley MacLaine (b. 1934), actress, New Age author, and sister of Warren Beatty

Pearl Bailey (1918–1990), singer, actress, and goodwill ambassador

Russell Baker (b. 1925), Pulitzer Prize–winning author of *Growing Up* and PBS host

Jack Beal (b. 1931), realist painter known for his murals

Nell Blaine (1922–1996), Impressionist painter

Mother Maybelle Carter (1909–1978), Grand Ole Opry star

Willa Cather (1873–1947), author of such novels as *My Antonia* and *Death Comes for the Archbishop*

Patsy Cline (1932–1963), groundbreaking country singer

Ella Fitzgerald (1917–1996), "First Lady of Song," immortal swing and jazz vocalist

Douglas Southall Freeman (1886–1953), two-time Pulitzer Prize–winning biographer

Ellen Glasgow (1873–1945), Pulitzer Prize–winning novelist

Emmet Gowin (b. 1941), fine art photographer

Thomas Jefferson (1743–1826), third U.S. president, author of the Declaration of Independence

Robert E. Lee (1807–1870), Civil War commander of Confederate forces

James Madison (1751–1836), fourth U.S. president

Sally Mann (b. 1951), avant-garde photographer

John Marshall (1755–1835), fourth chief justice of the U.S. Supreme Court, known as the "Great Chief Justice"

James Monroe (1758–1831), fifth U.S. president and author of the Monroe Doctrine

Wayne Newton (b. 1942), popular singer and Las Vegas performer

Walter Reed (1851–1902), army bacteriologist who discovered source of yellow fever

William Styron (b. 1925), Pulitzer Prize–winning novelist

Zachary Taylor (1784–1850), 12th U.S. president

Cy Twombly (b. 1928), internationally acclaimed artist

John Tyler (1790–1862), 10th U.S. president

Booker T. Washington (1856–1915), African-American educator

George Washington (1732–1799), first U.S. president

Woodrow Wilson (1856–1924), 28th U.S. president and Nobel Peace Prize laureate

Tom Wolfe (b. 1931), force behind New Journalism and critically acclaimed author

...and Great Places

Some interesting derivations of Virginia place names.

Assawoman An Indian name meaning many hills.

Bowling Green Named for the original estate of the Englishman who settled the area in 1670.

Broadway A town of rowdies whose name derived from the 19th-century term for a disreputable place, whose frequenters were on the "broadway" to dissolution.

Calfpasture, Cowpasture, and Bullpasture Rivers All derived their names from their popularity with the bovine set.

Charlottesville Named for King George III's queen and mother of George IV.

Delmarva Peninsula Named after the three states that form it: Delaware, Maryland, and Virginia.

Fairy Stone State Park Named for the local staurolite crystals that are considered lucky.

Falls Church Named for both the town's location on the falls of the Potomac and an Episcopal church built in 1734.

Front Royal British officers drilling troops near a large royal oak in this northern Piedmont town ordered their men to "front the royal."

Grottoes Named for the Grottoes Caverns in the center of town.

Hawksbill A 4,049-foot mountain in Shenandoah National Park shaped like a hawk's head and bill.

Lebanon A biblical reference inspired by an abundance of local cedars.

Luray Named either for an early blacksmith, Lewis Ray, or for the Lorraine region of France.

Newport News Derived from the riverside store established by colonial captain Christoper Newport, where the latest news could be had.

Northern Neck The northernmost Virginia peninsula, or neck.

Old Point Comfort End of peninsula between Hampton Roads and the Bay, whose harbor and deep channel offer "good comfort."

Richmond Named by William Byrd for England's Richmond-upon-Thames.

Stingray Point Where colonial hero John Smith was poisoned by the whipping tail of a stingray.

Troutdale Named for the excellent trout fishing in its Fox Creek.

Urbanna The English Queen Anne's "urb" or town.

Virginila Border town whose name derives from a combining of Virginia and North Carolina.

Appomattox An Algonquian word meaning a curving estuary.

VIRGINIA BY THE SEASONS
A Perennial Calendar of Events and Festivals

*Here is a selective listing of events that take place each year in the months noted;
we suggest calling ahead to local chambers of commerce for dates and details.*

January

Lexington
Historic Birthday Parties
Townwide events for Confederate generals Robert E. Lee and Stonewall Jackson, both former residents of this valley town.

Newport News
Wildlife Arts Festival
Works of art feature Virginia wildlife and scenery.

February

Alexandria
George Washington Birthday Celebration
Parade and events held throughout this historic colonial seaport.

Richmond
Maymont Flower and Garden Show
Held in the city coliseum, this show attracts nursery folks, landscape designers, and gardeners throughout the mid-Atlantic.

March

Charlottesville
Virginia Festival of the Book
At locations around the city, readings and discussions with local and nationally known writers celebrate the book.

Highland County
Maple Festival
Mountain festival of maple sap collecting and sugar-making; country music and cooking.

April

Norfolk
International Azalea Festival
Held at the city's renowned botanical gardens.

Southeastern Coast
Virginia Waterfront International Arts Festival
This Spoleto-like event takes in a 50-square-mile region and features internationally known performers.

Statewide
Historic Garden Week
Historic and contemporary homes and gardens open for the peak of spring bloom.

May

Arlington
Memorial Day
Ceremonies at Arlington National Cemetery.

Leesburg
Sheep Dog Trials and Farm Days
Held on the grounds of the antebellum Oaklands.

New Market
Reenactment of the Battle of New Market
Held on the 1864 Civil War battlefield.

The Plains
Virginia Gold Cup
One of the nation's premier steeplechases, in the heart of Virginia horse country.

Reedsville
Watermen's Heritage Weekend
This old watermen's town celebrates the bay's fisherfolk, oystermen, and crabbers.

Upperville
Hunt Country Stable Tour
Tours of thoroughbred breeding and training farms as well as private estates.

Winchester
Shenandoah Apple Blossom Festival

June

Hampton
Afrikan American Festival
Featuring music, performances, and food.
Hampton Jazz Festival
Features nationally known musicians.

Lynchburg
James River Batteau Festival
Re-creations of historic river batteaus depart here for a downriver trip to Richmond.

Norfolk
Harborfest
One of the East's largest waterfront festivals, featuring entertainers and exhibits.

The Plains
Vintage Virginia Wine Festival
Sample wares from the state's
burgeoning wine industry.

Wytheville
Chautauqua in the Park
A weeklong camp meeting
with entertainment.

July

Abingdon
Virginia Highlands Festival
Mountain heritage is celebrated
in music, crafts, and food in this
Shenandoah town.

Alexandria
Virginia Scottish Games
On the venerable grounds of
Episcopal High School, kilt-
wearing athletes compete in
traditional Scottish sports.

Chincoteague
*Annual Wild Pony Swim
and Auction*
Made famous by the book and
movie *Misty of Chincoteague*, the
event features a pony swim
across a narrow channel and a
public auction of the animals.

Orkney Springs
Shenandoah Valley Music Festival
Folk and big-band music are
featured on weekends from late
July through mid-August at the
historic Shrinemont Resort.

August

Galax
Old Fiddlers' Convention
The oldest and biggest fiddlers'
convention in the East.

Hampton
Hampton Cup Regatta
The country's oldest and largest
hydroplane powerboat race.

Roanoke
Virginia Mountain Peach Festival
Crafts, entertainers, and food
celebrate the peach.

September

Chincoteague
Decoy Carvers Association Show
Famous island carvers show
off their decoys.

Richmond
*NASCAR Miller Genuine
Draft 400*
Virginia State Fair

October

Charlottesville
Virginia Film Festival
Screens classical and contemporary films and offers discussions
and seminars.

Ferrum
Blue Ridge Folklife Festival
Devoted to the old-time tradi-
tions and heritage of the Blue
Ridge Mountains.

Roanoke
Roanoke Railway Festival
The Virginia Museum of
Transportation revisits trains.

Waterford
*Waterford Homes Tour and
Crafts Exhibit*
One of the East's most popular
crafts exhibitions, held in a
charming Quaker village.

November

Charles City County
Virginia's First Thanksgiving
At historic Berkeley Plantation
on the James, the first Thanksgiving, celebrated by colonists in
1619, is reenacted. Cruises from
Richmond access the event.

Mount Vernon
Mount Vernon by Candlelight
For three weekends, George
Washington's Potomac River
estate is decorated for the season
and lit by candles.

Tazewell
A Pioneer Thanksgiving
Held at the re-created log settle-
ment at Historic Crab Orchard
Museum.

Urbanna
Urbanna Oyster Festival

December

Alexandria
Scottish Christmas Walk
A fife-and-drum parade and
citywide festivities.

Colonial Williamsburg
Grand Illumination
The holiday scene is heralded
in colonial style.

WHERE TO GO
Museums, Attractions, Gardens, and Other Arts Resources

Call for seasons and hours when open.

Museums

CHRYSLER MUSEUM
245 W. Olney Rd., Norfolk, 804-622-1211
One of the country's finest small museums, features Greco–Roman, Egyptian, and pre-Columbian artifacts; American paintings; and art glass.

GADSBY'S TAVERN MUSEUM
134 N. Royal St., Alexandria, 703-838-4242
Colonial/early Federal tavern dating from the time of George Washington.

LEE–FENDALL HOUSE MUSEUM
614 Oronoco St., Alexandria, 703-548-1789
Home of prominent Lee family for several generations and later home of labor boss John L. Lewis; furnishings reflect both periods.

THE MARINERS' MUSEUM
100 Museum Dr., Newport News, 757-591-7320
Exhibits of nautical artifacts include a working steam engine, vintage boats, and ship models.

MUSEUM AND WHITE HOUSE OF THE CONFEDERACY
1201 E. Clay St., Richmond, 804-649-1861
Museum features Confederate artifacts and paintings; the adjacent restored Victorian house was used by Confederate President Jefferson Davis.

EDGAR ALLAN POE MUSEUM
1914–16 E. Main St., Richmond, 804-648-5523
Housed in Richmond's oldest home, features a collection of Poe memorabilia and writings.

ABBY ALDRICH ROCKEFELLER FOLK ART CENTER
Williamsburg, 757-220-7645 or 800-HISTORY
One of the premier collections of American folk art.

VALENTINE MUSEUM AND 1812 WICKHAM HOUSE
1015 E. Clay St., Richmond, 804-649-0711
Museum features changing exhibits and archives on Richmond's history; restored Wickham house is a model of Federal-style decor.

VIRGINIA HISTORICAL SOCIETY: THE MUSEUM OF VIRGINIA HISTORY
428 N. Blvd., Richmond, 804-358-4901
Changing and long-term exhibits showcase Virginia history.

VIRGINIA MUSEUM OF FINE ARTS
2800 Grove Ave., Richmond, 804-367-0844
Exhibits world art from ancient Egypt through the Classical era to the present; periodically sponsors exhibits highlighting Virginia artists.

Attractions

ARLINGTON NATIONAL CEMETERY
Arlington, 703-607-8052
Some 600 acres on Potomac bluffs include Tomb of the Unknowns, John F. Kennedy's gravesite, and Arlington House—former home of Robert and Mary Lee.

BARTER THEATRE
W. Main St., Abingdon, 540-628-3991
As State Theatre of Virginia, Barter has produced musicals and dramas for 65 seasons; complex now includes an experimental and children's theatre.

CAPE HENRY LIGHTHOUSES
Fort Story, off Rte. 60, Virginia Beach, 757-422-9421
Old lighthouse dates from 1791, newer one from 1881.

CHANCELLORSVILLE BATTLEFIELD
Visitor Center, Rte. 3, Fredericksburg, 540-786-2880
Site of Lee's greatest Civil War victory.

COLONIAL WILLIAMSBURG
Williamsburg, 757-220-7645 or 800-HISTORY
Renowned, restored colonial town on 173 acres.

FORT MONROE
Fort Monroe, 757-727-3391
America's only moat-encircled fort still in use; site of
1802 Old Point Comfort Lighthouse.

JAMESTOWN NATIONAL HISTORICAL PARK
East end of Colonial Pkwy., Yorktown, 757-229-1733
Site of first permanent English settlement in America
established in 1607; features visitor center, museum,
1639 church tower, and glasshouse.

JAMESTOWN SETTLEMENT
East end of Colonial Pkwy., Yorktown, 757-229-1607
Re-creations of 17th-century Powhatan village, fort
built by the first colonists, and their three ships.

MANASSAS NATIONAL BATTLEFIELD PARK
6511 Sudley Rd., Manassas, 703-361-1339
Site of two Civil War battles, including the first of the
war in 1861; also known as Bull Run.

RICHMOND NATIONAL BATTLEFIELD PARK
3215 E. Broad St., Richmond, 804-226-1981
Highlights McClellan's 1862 Peninsula campaign and
Grant's 1864 march through Virginia.

THEATER AT LIME KILN
14 S. Randolph St., Lexington, 540-463-3074
Features a stage of stone ruins in open air; original
dramas, including the acclaimed *Stonewall Country.*

UNIVERSITY OF VIRGINIA
Rte. 250 Bus., Charlottesville, 804-924-0311
Third U.S. president Thomas Jefferson founded his
"academical village" here in 1819; now a UNESCO
World Heritage Site.

WREN BUILDING
*College of William and Mary, Williamsburg,
757-221-1540*
Oldest U.S. college building features a colonial great
hall, chapel, and classroom.

Homes and Gardens

BELMONT, THE GARI MELCHERS ESTATE AND
MEMORIAL GALLERY
224 Washington St., Falmouth, 540-654-1015
Historic house and art studio belonging to the painter
Gari Melchers (1860–1932).

BERKELEY PLANTATION
*12602 Harrison Landing Rd., Charles City,
804-829-6018*
The James River's most historic plantation, home
to the Harrison family.

CARLYLE HOUSE
121 N. Fairfax St., Alexandria, 703-549-2997
The 18th-century Georgian home of landowner
and merchant John Carlyle.

EVELYNTON PLANTATION
*6701 John Tyler Memorial Hwy., Charles City,
800-473-5075*
Historic home of President John Tyler; decorated
in period furnishings.

LEWIS GINTER BOTANICAL GARDEN
1800 Lakeside Ave., Richmond, 804-262-9934
Features Flagler Perennial Garden, the Children's
Garden, West Island Garden, seasonal displays, Robins
Tea House, and historic Bloemendaal House.

GUNSTON HALL PLANTATION
10709 Gunston Rd., Lorton, 703-550-9220
The Potomac estate of colonial statesman George
Mason, noted for its woodwork and grounds.

KENMORE PLANTATION

1201 Washington Ave., Fredericksburg, 540-373-3381

Elegant mansion of George Washington's sister, Betty; famous for its plasterwork.

BOYHOOD HOME OF ROBERT E. LEE

607 Oronoco St., Alexandria, 703-548-8454

Built in 1795 and home to Lee from ages 5 to 18.

MAYMONT HOUSE

1700 Hampton St., Richmond, 804-358-7166

Elaborate Victorian home and gardens; renowned for its Swan Bed.

MONTICELLO: HOME OF THOMAS JEFFERSON

P.O. Box 316, Charlottesville, 804-984-9822

Jefferson's Classical Revival house features original furnishings and his inventions; grounds include period gardens and Jefferson's grave.

MONTPELIER

11407 Constitution Hwy., Montpelier Station, 540-672-2728

Home of President James Madison and his wife, Dolly, and subsequent estate of the Du Pont clan.

MORVEN PARK

Off Rte. 698, Leesburg, 703-777-2414

Classic Virginia hunt country estate; grounds feature carriage collection and fox-hunting museum.

NORFOLK BOTANICAL GARDEN

6700 Azalea Garden Rd., Norfolk, 757-441-5830

Situated on 155 acres, features more than 20 theme gardens; famous for its spring azalea display.

POPLAR FOREST

Poplar Forest Dr. and Old Foxhall Dr., Forest, 804-525-1806

Jefferson's very personal country villa; the interior is currently being restored.

SHIRLEY PLANTATION

501 Shirley Plantation Rd., Charles City, 800-232-1613

Circa 1613 home, still owned and occupied by descendants of original Hill and Carter families.

STRATFORD HALL PLANTATION

Rte. 214, Stratford, 804-493-8038

Imposing Georgian mansion that was the ancestral home of the Lee family and birthplace of Robert E. Lee.

MAGGIE WALKER NATIONAL HISTORIC SITE

3215 E. Broad St., Richmond, 804-771-2017

Victorian home of early 20th-century African-American leader and first woman founder of a bank.

GEORGE WASHINGTON'S MOUNT VERNON ESTATE AND GARDENS

South end of George Washington Memorial Pkwy., Mount Vernon, 703-780-0200

Situated on 500 acres, features the mansion of the first president; tombs of Washington and his wife, Martha; 2 museums; 12 outbuildings; gardens, and a pioneer farmer site.

WOODLAWN PLANTATION

9000 Richmond Hwy., Mount Vernon, 703-780-4000

Federal-style home of Martha Washington's granddaughter, Nelly Custis.

FRANK LLOYD WRIGHT'S POPE-LEIGHEY HOUSE

9000 Richmond Hwy., Mount Vernon, 703-780-4000

On the grounds of Woodlawn Plantation, an example of architect's modest Usonian homes.

Other Resources

CAPITOL OF VIRGINIA

9th and Grace Sts., Richmond, 804-786-4344

Designed by Thomas Jefferson, it houses Houdon's statue of George Washington surrounded by busts of Virginia-born U.S. presidents.

CREDITS

The authors have made every effort to reach copyright holders of text and owners of illustrations, and wish to thank those individuals and institutions that permitted the reprinting of text or the reproduction of works in their collections. Credits not listed in the captions are provided below. References are to page numbers; the designations a, b, and c indicate position of illustrations on pages.

Text

Dietz Press: From *What Is It About Virginia?* by Guy Friddell. Copyright © 1966 by Guy Friddell. Reprinted with permission.

HarperCollins: From *Pilgrim at Tinker Creek* by Annie Dillard. Copyright © 1974 by Annie Dillard. Reprinted with permission.

NTC/Contemporary Publishing Group, Inc.: From *Growing Up* by Russell Baker. Copyright © 1982 by Russell Baker. Used with permission.

Penguin Putnam, Inc.: Excerpt from the introduction by John Barth to *Beautiful Swimmers* by William W. Warner. Copyright © 1976, 1987 by William W. Warner.

Random House, Inc.: Lines from *John Brown's Body* by Stephen Vincent Benét. Copyright © 1928 by Stephen Vincent Benét. Reprinted by permission of Doubleday, a division of Random House. Excerpt from *A Tidewater Morning: Three Tales From Youth* by William Styron. Copyright © 1993 by William Styron. Reprinted with permission.

Illustrations

ABBY ALDRICH ROCKEFELLER FOLK ART CENTER, COLONIAL WILLIAMSBURG: **1** *Washington and Lafayette*. Oil on canvas. 22¼ x 33⅞"; **67b** Mrs. Seth Wilkinson, c. 1825–30. Artist unknown. Oil on yellow poplar panel. 30 x 25½"; AMERICA HURRAH ARCHIVE, NEW YORK: **13a** Fox hound quilt, c. 1950s. Cotton. 71 x 85"; **69b** House-and-tree quilt, c. 1900. Cotton. 78 x 78"; AMERICAN HARVESTER/CORBIS-BETTMANN: **40** *Steeles Tavern* by N. C. Wyeth, c. 1920s; BELMONT, THE GARI MELCHERS ESTATE AND MEMORIAL GALLERY, MARY WASHINGTON COLLEGE, FREDRICKSBURG, VIRGINIA: **82** *In Old Virginia* by Gari Melchers, c. 1918. Oil on canvas. 32 x 40"; THE BRIDGEMAN ART LIBRARY INTERNATIONAL, LTD.: **15a** Sir Walter Raleigh. Private Collection; **31** Early map of

Virginia. Hand-colored engraving. British Library, London; **34b** Indian peace medal, 1776. British Museum, London; BROWN BROTHERS, STERLING, PENNSYLVANIA: **88** Shirley MacLaine; CHRISTIE'S IMAGES: **24** *On the Shenandoah*. Oil on canvas. 30 x 54"; **36b** Weathervane. Painted sheet metal. 18 x 56"; **49b** *A Liberated Woman*. Oil on canvas. 42 x 32"; **55** *Summer in the Blue Ridge*. Oil on canvas. 30 x 54½"; **62** *Mount Vernon from the West*. Oil on canvas. 21¾ x 35½"; CORBIS: **16b** George Washington statue. Photo Buddy Mays; **22b, 42, 56, 57b;** CORCORAN GALLERY OF ART, WASHINGTON, D.C.: **38b** *The Old Westover Mansion* by Edward Lamson Henry, 1869. Oil on panel. 11¼ x 14⅝". Photo Corbis-Bettmann. DAVID DAVID GALLERY, PHILADELPHIA: **36a** *Drummer Boy* by Julian Scott, 1891. Oil on canvas. 20 x 25"; PIETER ESTERSOHN/ LACHAPELLE REPRESENTS: **63a** Footbridge; **63a** Khan residence; FOLIO, INC.: **21b, 45a** NASA launch. Photo Michael R. Brown; **45b, 51a** Mennonite buggy. Photo Everett Johnson; **52a, 52b, 61** The University of Virginia. Photo Ted Hooper; **64a** Dining room at Gunston Hall. John Skowronski; **64b** Chatham Manor. Photo Patricia Lanza; **65b** Pope—Leighey House. Photo John Skowronski; **67a, 72a, 80b, 87b** Luray Caverns. Photo Dennis Johnson; BARON AND ELLIN B. GORDON: **85a** *George Washington* by Anderson Johnson, c. 1985. Acrylic on composition board. 22⅛ x 16⅞". Photo Tom Green; THE GRANGER COLLECTION, NEW YORK: **33b** Woodcut of tobacco, 1576; **41a** *The End of the Hunt*. Oil on canvas; **59** Nat Turner. Color engraving, c. late 1800s; HALL OF VALOR, CIVIL WAR MUSEUM, NEW MARKET: **17, 57a** Memorial to the Virginia cadets. Stained glass. 9 x 29". Both photos, Catherine Karnow/Woodfin Camp & Associates, Inc., New York; HAMPTON UNIVERSITY MUSEUM: **86c** *Fish* by Robert Howell, 1996. Paint on wood and metal with plastic. 69½ x 62½ x 19". Gift of Baron and Ellin B. Gordon. Photo Tom Green; V. W. JOYNER COMPANY: **70b** Smithfield ham label. Collection Peter D. Pruden, III; LIBRARY OF CONGRESS: **16a, 49a** Pocahontas tobacco label; **38a** *Lee in Richmond* by Matthew Brady, 1865; LIBRARY OF VIRGINIA, RICHMOND: **28** A Virginia Algonquian. Engraving. 10¼ x 8¾"; **29** Village of Pomiooc. Engraving. 13¾ x 8⅔"; **30b** *Smith Rescued by Pocahontas*. Tinted lithograph. 17¾ x 24"; **33a** Young George Washington; **35** Patrick Henry. Engraving by Alfred Jones; **37** *The Monitor and the Merrimack*. Engraving; **48** Coal miners; **58a** Governor Douglas Wilder; **58b** Senator Harry Byrd and family; MAIER MUSEUM OF ART, RANDOLPH-

MACON WOMAN'S COLLEGE, LYNCHBURG, VIRGINIA: **19** *Dismal Swamp* by Flavius J. Fisher. Oil on canvas. 30 x 50". Gift of Mrs. Robert N. Winfree, 1976; THE MARINERS' MUSEUM, NEWPORT NEWS: **13c** Pitcher featuring Virginia's seal. Ceramic. 9½ x 4½–6"; **20b** Horseshoe crab. Watercolor on paper. 12 x 17⅛"; **23** *Mary of Norfolk*. Watercolor on paper. 5⅞ x 9⅜"; **43** *Watermen*. Bodine Collection; **44** Hampton Roads. Lithograph; MAYMONT FOUNDATION: **86b** Swan bed. Photo Richard Cheek; MONTICELLO/THOMAS JEFFERSON MEMORIAL FOUNDATION, INC.: **60b** Jefferson's Cabinet; **63b** Goblet by Claude-Nicolas Delanoy. Silver with gilt interior. 4⅝" h. Photo Edward Owen; THE MUSEUM OF THE CONFEDERACY, RICHMOND: **2** *The Last Meeting of Lee and Jackson* by E. B. D. Julio, 1869. Oil on canvas. 102 x 74"; MUSEUM OF EARLY SOUTHERN DECORATIVE ARTS, WINSTON-SALEM, NORTH CAROLINA: **27** *The Natural Bridge*. Aquatint by J. C. Stadler, 1808, after William Roberts. Ink on paper. 32¼ x 24½"; WALLACE NALL: **74** *The Hunt*, 1978. Acrylic on canvas. 20 x 24"; NATIONAL GEOGRAPHIC SOCIETY IMAGE COLLECTION: **10, 12a** State flag. Illustration by Marilyn Dye Smith; **12b** Cardinal and dogwood. Illustration by Robert E. Hynes; NATIONAL PORTRAIT GALLERY, SMITHSONIAN INSTITUTION, WASHINGTON, D.C.: **30a** Pocahontas, after an engraving by Simon van de Passe. Oil on canvas. 30¼ x 24⅛"; **60a** *Thomas Jefferson* by Gilbert Stuart, 1805. Oil on canvas. Photo The Granger Collection, New York; THE OGDEN MUSEUM OF SOUTHERN ART, UNIVERSITY OF NEW ORLEANS: **75** *Midway*. Oil on board. 16 x 20"; **85b** *Main Street, Tazewell, Virginia*. Oil on masonite. 14½ x 16½"; PHOTOFEST: **79** Still from *The X-Files*. © 1995 Fox Broadcasting; PRIVATE COLLECTION: **13b** "Carry Me Back to Old Virginny" sheet music; REYNOLDS GALLERY, RICHMOND: **5** *Untitled* by Javier Tapia, 1998. Watercolor on paper. 66 x 54". Collection the artist; **21a** *Dunes at Dusk* by Stephen Fox, 1998. Oil on linen, mounted on panel. 12 x 23"; **50** *The Moaners Bench* by Julien Binford, c. 1941. Oil on canvas. 24 x 34". Collection the estate of Julien Binford; **83b** *Living Room* by Philip Geiger, 1998. Oil on panel. 32 x 24". Collection the artist; **84a** *Barriers* by Stephen Fox, 1996–97. Oil on canvas. 59 x 60". Collection the artist; **84b** *Jazz Abstraction* by Nell Blaine, 1946–47. Oil on paper. 18 x 12". Collection the estate of the artist; MICHAEL SKOTT: **12c** Oyster; SMITHSONIAN INSTITUTION, ARCHIVES OF AMERICAN GARDENS: **73** Rose arbor at Chatham. Hand-tinted lantern slide; HARRIET SPURLIN: **76a** Russell

Baker; **76b** Annie Dillard. Both photos, Thomas Victor; MRS. ADELE STERN: **80a** *Musicians*. Oil on corrugated board. 7¾ x 10¼"; THE STOCK MARKET: **89** Appomattox. © 1999 Chromosohm/Sohm; THEATRE AT LIME KILN: **78a**; CY TWOMBLY GALLERY, THE MENIL COLLECTION, HOUSTON: **83a** *Untitled* by Cy Twombly, 1954. Wood, glass, mirrors, fabric, twine, wire, wooden spoons, oil crayon, house paint, wax. 80 x 13⅞". Photo Hickey-Robertson, Houston; UNIVERSITY OF CALIFORNIA LIBRARY, DAVIS, DEPARTMENT OF SPECIAL COLLECTIONS: **72b** Seed catalog cover; USPS: **81b** Patsy Cline postage stamp ® and © 1993 U.S. Postal Service. All rights reserved; VALENTINE MUSEUM, RICHMOND: **9** *Mann S. Valentine and the Artist*. Oil on canvas. Diameter: 24¼"; **66b** Woodwork; VIRGINIA MUSEUM OF FINE ARTS, RICHMOND: **34a** *George Washington and General Rochambeau*. Oil on wooden panel. 10¾ x 15". Gift of Mrs. Preston Davie. Photo Katherine Wetzel; **39** *Winter Quarters, Culpeper, Virginia*. Oil on canvas. 12 x 18". Gift of Edgar William and Bernice Chrysler Garbisch. Photo Ron Jennings; **53** *Dismal Swamp Canal*. Oil on wood panel. 11 x 15". Gift of Eugene B. Sydnor, Jr. Photo Ron Jennings; **86a** Imperial Czarevitch Easter Egg by Peter Carl Fabergé, 1912. Lapis lazuli, gold, diamonds. 5 x 3½". Bequest of Lillian Thomas Pratt. Photo Katherine Wetzel; All photos, © Virginia Museum of Fine Arts; VIRGINIA TOURISM CORPORATION: **14a, 46b, 87a** Ship replica at Jamestown. Photo Len Kaufman; **87c** Virginia Beach outdoor sculpture. Photo A & C Purcell; WINTERTHUR MUSEUM, DELAWARE: **69a** Tureen and cover, c. 1786. Porcelain hardpaste. 4⅞ x 4¾". Gift of Henry F. du Pont.

Acknowledgments

Walking Stick Press wishes to thank our project staff: Miriam Lewis, Joanna Lynch, Thérèse Martin, Laurie Donaldson, Inga Lewin, Kristi Hein, and Mark Woodworth.

For other assistance with Virginia, we are especially grateful to: Laurel Anderson/Photosynthesis, Natalie Goldstein, Jan Hughes, Ellin B. Gordon, Audrey C. Johnson of the Library of Virginia, Beverly Reynolds of Reynolds Gallery, Claudia Jew at the Mariners' Museum, the staff of the Virginia Museum of Fine Art, Lorraine Dunn at the Virginia Beach Department of Convention and Visitor Development, and Julie Grimes, Pamela Jewell, Martha Steger, and Jay Holloman at the Virginia Tourism Corporation.